MARY:
GOD'S SUPREME
MASTERPIECE

MARY:
GOD'S SUPREME
MASTERPIECE

Fr. Bartholomew Gottemoller, O.C.S.O.

Queenship
PUBLISHING COMPANY
P.O Box 42028 Santa Barbara, CA 93140-2028
(800)647-9882 Fax: (805) 569-3274

NIHIL OBSTAT
        Father Colin F. Bircumshaw
        Censor Librorum

IMPRIMATUR
        Most Reverend George H. Niederauer, Ph.D.
        Bishop of Salt Lake City
        November 22, 1995

Library of Congress Number: 95-69784

ISBN: 1-882972-48-1

Published by:
        Queenship Publishing
        P.O. Box 42028
        Santa Barbara, CA 93140-2028
        (800) 647-9882 FAX: (805) 569-3274

Printed in the United States of America

Contents

PREFACE

In one sense this is not the book I originally intended to write, and in another sense it is. Originally I wanted to write a book on *The Plan of God*. However, once I started writing, I soon found myself confronted with Mary's place in God's plan, something I had not yet clarified in my own mind. It was then that I came to realize that first I would have to write a book about Mary before I could adequately treat of God's plan for his creation.

Now that I have found Mary's place, I find that everything I knew before of God's plan falls very neatly into place. So much so that there is nothing more of importance I can add in writing about God's plan save to enlarge on certain details such as the nature of grace, the sacraments, the gifts of the Holy Spirit and the like. I could well use as a subtitle for this book the title I had first intended, *The Plan of God*.

Mystery in God: When we speak of God and Mary we must know that we are entering into the territory of mystery. Our understanding of God's works must ever remain limited, for as St. Paul says, "Who could know the mind of the Lord? Who could ever be his counselor?" (Rom. 11:34) The fact that God and Mary are enveloped in mystery does not mean. that we can know little or nothing about them or that there is no value in seeking greater knowledge of them. St. Thomas Aquinas says, "Imperfect knowledge of what is highest is better than perfect knowledge of what is lowest." To know God imperfectly is better than knowing a stone perfectly. To have an imperfect knowledge of the workings of an atom is better than perfect knowledge of the working of a clock.

In studying God and his works we cannot avoid mystery. Indeed a religion that does not admit of mystery cannot be from God, but of necessity is an invention of man. We find mystery in every field of knowledge and in the material world around us. If there is mystery in what God has made, we should expect to find it still more in God himself: in his inner life and in his plan for creation.

The need of symbols: What makes our understanding of God and of religious truths more difficult is that they are spiritual realities. Modern-day man, especially, is so taken up with the material world around him, that he is inclined to think that nothing exists that is not matter. But spiritual realities do exist, and they are even higher in nature and greater in value than all material things. Our difficulty with spiritual realities springs from the fact that we can form no direct concept of a spirit. The only way we can envision a spirit is as a power: something you cannot see but which can produce a sensible effect, as for example, radiation or electricity. Because of this, when we speak of spiritual or religious truths we have to use material symbols, metaphors, comparisons, and parables.

In this book I will concentrate on comparisons, using two kinds: social comparisons, such as the family, and organic comparisons, like the vine and its branches. Social comparisons will help us see our union with God as a person-to-person relationship, while organic comparisons will help us see the closeness of that relationship as being a living unity.

Since, as they say, "All comparisons limp," we must not take comparisons in too literal a sense or apply them to something beyond that particular point they are being used to clarify.

Our call to share God's life: God's only reason for creating is to share his life and happiness with others. Being infinitely perfect and Lacking nothing, God can only act in order to share of his fullness. Also, whatever God does must be done with absolute perfection, nor can he be thwarted in this by any creature, not even by the free will of man. Then too, the means God uses to achieve his goal must be the very best. If there were some more perfect way, he would have to use it, otherwise he would not be the all-perfect God, Hence, with regard to his goal, of sharing his life and happiness with mankind, God must achieve this in the most perfect possible way, wholly worthy of his infinite wisdom, power and goodness.

The purpose of this book is to show how God has actually achieved this, his goal, in the most perfect way possible, through Jesus and Mary. In Jesus' *active* redemption, God has offered to man everything he can possibly share with his intellectual creature. And in Mary's *passive* redemption, a mere creature has freely and fully received and accepted all that a creature is capable of receiving from God. And now we, all mankind, are being offered to share in their absolute perfection according to our union with them in charity. Our degree of charity determines our capacity to receive of their fullness.

In Mary is found all the life and happiness God can give a mere creature and all that a mere creature is capable of receiving. Mary is God's SUPREME MASTERPIECE and, being our Mother, she wants to share with us, her children, that fullness of God's life and happiness we are capable of receiving, "This is a work of the Lord and it is wonderful in our eyes." (Ps. 117:23)

INTRODUCTION

When we look at the created world around us we find marvels and beauties both in the great and small, that are overwhelming in their reality. In the heavens we find a vastness that extends for billions of light years in every direction and which is so full of galaxies and stars that the earth on which we live appears as a speck of dust in the vast ocean of space. We find the same vastness, but in reverse, in the living cell and in the atom. In these we find marvels just as incomprehensible in their smallness as the universe is in its greatness. Our technology falls short of ways to penetrate fully into the vastness of these two realms of reality so that we are left in wonder, not only at what we actually find therein, but still more at what we realize is beyond our grasp.

Great as the material world is, man himself is an even greater marvel especially by reason of his intellectual life, which sets him apart and above all the rest of the material creation. Man* has the capacity to know everything that exists or can exist and this capacity is limited only by his mode of knowing, namely, through intellectual concepts derived from the things he sees or experiences around him. What man can know in this way and what he can express and create through such concepts has filled libraries with books beyond all reckoning. By using what God has put into his creation, man, by his mental powers and technology, can make

---

* The term "Man" is used here and frequently throughout this book to mean, the human being without distinction of sex. This is the first meaning given in the dictionary and for lack of a better word, I have found its use unavoidable.

many wonderful things, like radios, TV sets, computers, space crafts and all our modern inventions.

Besides knowledge, man also has the power of free-will which finds its fullest expression in love. He can freely enter into a loving friendship with other people and even with God himself. Love is truly the source of man's highest joy. He experiences it in the family, in romance and in every kind of friendship and relationship with other people. Love is the moving power of life; we cannot live without it.

God's works must be absolutely perfect: If the universe itself and man are so great, how much greater must not God be. God cannot give what he does not have. God has to be at least as good and desirable as all the created goods he has given us. Indeed there is so much power, wisdom and beauty revealed in creation that we are forced to acknowledge that its creator must be far greater than all he has made, including man himself. Man may be the greatest of God's works in the visible world, but he certainly does not exhaust the scope of God's creative power.

So great is the perfection of everything God has made that we can only conclude that God must be unlimited in wisdom and power. Hence, whatever God does, considering the end he has in view, has to be done with the greatest possible perfection. If there were a better way to achieve his goal God would have to choose it, otherwise he would not be God: the supreme being.

From this it follows that there must be some point wherein God's creation reaches its highest possible perfection so that even God could not make it more perfect. As we shall see, the purpose or goal God has in view for his creation is to share his own divine life and happiness with his intellectual creatures in the highest possible way. Now that highest possible sharing of his divine life and happiness with a mere creature is to be found in Mary of Nazareth, the mother of Jesus.

It is true that Jesus, the God-man, is the greatest effect of God's creative power, but Jesus is not a mere creature, for he is divine in his person. Mary, therefore, stands out among all mere creatures as God's Supreme Masterpiece. In her alone God's creation has reached its highest peak of perfection. As the poet has said, "She is our tainted nature's solitary boast."

Mary's definition of herself: When Mary was asked by Bernadete at Lourdes who she was, Mary answered, "I am the Immaculate Conception." Here Mary did not say, I am she who was immaculately conceived, but "I am the Immaculate Conception." She appears to be giving us a definition of herself, somewhat as God gave a definition of himself when he said to Moses, "I am who Am," that is, "The Self-existing Being" wholly distinct from all other things which exist only by him.

St. Maximilian Kolbe was deeply impressed by these words of Mary and sought to understand their full meaning. Seeing that the fruit of human love is the conception of a child, he saw that the fruit of God's divine Love must also be a conception, the Holy Spirit. Mary then, as the *Immaculate Conception*, must be closely related to the Holy Spirit, a kind of created image of the Holy Spirit, a likeness of God's love or motherliness.

While Jesus is a created revelation of God's Paternity it would appear very appropriate that Mary should be a created revelation of God's Maternity, but of course without being a divine person. Mary completes God's created revelation of himself as possessing the qualities of both male and female.

There must be a close relationship between Mary and the Holy Spirit, but it is a mystery which the human mind may never be able to penetrate. Here then, I would like to offer a simpler approach to our understanding of Mary as the Immaculate Conception: that she is the embodiment of *God's concept* of the most perfect creature, a *concept* of one who is so immaculate and perfect that even God could not make a more perfect creature, at least, according to his present order of creation. As a creature Mary is uniquely "The Immaculate Conception." I would like to say that Mary is absolutely the most perfect possible creature God could ever make, but, since we cannot know the full possibility of God's creative power, we have to avoid stating something we cannot really know.

Although Jesus, as man, is God's greatest creative work, he is not a *mere creature* for he is divine in person. Indeed it is just because he is both human and divine that he is our one and only Mediator with God. But if Jesus is our perfect Mediator with God, Mary is our perfect Mediatrix with Jesus; she unites us perfectly with Jesus as man even as Jesus, as God, unites us perfectly with his Father. Mary then, clearly has a unique place in God's plan of creations and the Catholic faithful have always sensed this down the centuries with an ever increasing devotion to Mary. If at times their devotion has appeared to be exaggerated, to the scandal of those outside the church, this simply attests to the fact that what God has made Mary to be in spiritual beauty and holiness, is so far above our human understanding that we cannot give her too much honor short of what is due to God alone.

Division of subject matter: My purpose in this book will be to show, not only how Mary is God's supreme masterpiece, but also how God has willed to bring his whole creation into unity with himself through Jesus and Mary in the most perfect possible way, wholly worthy of God's infinite wisdom, power and goodness. Only through Jesus and Mary can we ourselves attain to that perfect unity with God which even God could not make more perfect according to his present plan for creation.

I am dividing this book into three parts. **Part I**: deals with the principles of reason and faith that should guide us in our understanding of Mary's place in God's plan. In **Part II**: I want to reflect on the life of Mary, to see how these principles of reason and faith have been fully realized in Mary. In **Part III**: I want to show how Mary, as a mere creature, is indeed God's supreme masterpiece and how, by uniting ourselves with Jesus and Mary, we and all creation are taken up into God so that his great work of creation and redemption will eventually reach a state of absolute perfection in unity with God himself.

PART I

THE GENERAL PRINCIPLES
OF REASON AND FAITH
IN MARIOLOGY

INTRODUCTION

Mary *is a creature*. That is the most basic principle in our understanding of Mary. There can be no question, then, of giving Mary any divine prerogative. Since, however, God can do more than we can understand, we must not be surprised to find that God has filled Mary with such greatness and spiritual beauty that she appears to us with a glory close to being divine. The fact that Mary is a creature postulates that she has a creator and that therefore God exists, that he had a reason for creating, and a goal for Mary, and indeed, for all mankind and creation itself. All this we can know to some degree from creation itself through our human reason, and it is something we must look into.

Through divine revelation, on the other hand, we can know much more about God and his inner life and also about his purpose in creating man and the world: that he has actually willed to call man to a personal union of friendship with himself. This is something we could never know through creation. Our source for this knowledge is the Bible, both the Old Testament and the New Testament. Therein we find God indicating his plan and will for mankind by freely offering his divine friendship to mankind in our first parents, Adam and Eve. But they, refusing to accept it, incurred the guilt of original sin, and thus lost God's friendship for all their descendants: the future human race. However, God promised to send mankind a savior who would redeem man and win back God's offer of friendship. This he fulfilled in the New Testament through Jesus Christ, the Incarnate Son of God, with whom Mary was to be closely associated.

Division of subject matter: Here in **Part I**, I would like to consider what pertains to Mary in the order of creation and then what pertains to her in the order of divine revelation. In the order of divine revelation I will first look at Mary as foreshadowed in the Old Testament and then as wonderfully associated with Jesus in his redeeming work in the New Testament. I will also consider Mary's role in the early Church after Jesus' departure by his Ascension. I will conclude by considering Mary's Assumption into heaven and her present role in the world as the Mediatrix of all graces.

In the first chapter, of this part, I may appear to be speaking very little about Mary, but I trust my readers will be patient. I will be clarifying some truths that will help us later on to better understand Mary's place in God's plan.

CHAPTER I

MARY IN THE ORDER
OF CREATION

A) EXISTENCE OF GOD

Mary is a human being and hence a creature like ourselves. She did not and could not make herself; she needed a creator. Mankind has generally believed in the existence of some supreme being or beings as the source of all that exists in the world. We cannot help but recognize that everything in our world is contingent, that of itself it cannot exist. Hence some outside first cause had to give it existence. But our mind also tells us that such a first cause *must always exist*, otherwise it would require another cause to give it existence, and then another, until we came to some cause that simply always existed; one whose very nature is to exist.

What that cause might be, we have only two possible choices: either God, the most perfect in being or *matter*, the most imperfect in being. In our experience, however, it is always the more perfect that precedes the less perfect. But in both we have the question, "How can something always exist."

How something can always exist: Human reason can give no direct answer to that question, even though it can tell us that, if such a cause did not exist, nothing would now exist. We must accept it on faith: a faith based on what we see existing before our eyes: a contingent universe that can not make itself. We have to humble ourselves and recognize that we are limited creatures.

We are limited even as animals are limited. The animal is limited in that it cannot understand our intellectual life of science and literature, but our intellectual life does not cease to exist because of that. We too are limited in that we cannot understand how God can always exist, but that does not destroy his reality. God is much higher above us than we are above the animal. We have no way of forming a concept of something that always exists and yet, what we see around us, requires such a cause. We must accept that cause as being superior to ourselves even as we are superior to the animal.

To suppose that mere matter could be that self-existing cause, evolving by chance into ever more perfect forms, is simply irrational. Mere chance can no more produce order and physical laws than a tornado, hitting a junk yard, could produce an airplane regardless how long it blows. If matter could evolve into more perfect forms, it could only be because their intelligent creator had put that capacity into matter. However, we have no clear scientific proof that God has given matter that capacity.

A higher world of reality: We have to admit that there exists a world of reality far higher than our own intellectual world even as we are higher than the animal world. Nor should we be surprised at our inability to understand how God can always exist. Even in our material world there are many things that are beyond our full understanding. For example, where are the boundaries of the universe and, where they are, what is beyond them? We cannot begin to imagine either of the only two possible answers, namely, that the universe has no boundaries or that there is nothing beyond them. When we see the wisdom and power God has revealed in the marvels our universe, both in the big and small and in what he has made man to be, we can only stand in awe at what God must be like in himself.

Spiritual realities: The existence of God brings up another problem. No one has ever seen God with their bodily eyes because he is said to be a spirit. But how do we know that spiritual realities really exist? Here again we have to admit the limitations of our knowing powers. However, we have solid grounds for admitting the existence of spiritual realities and even that they are higher and of much more value than any material realities. Certainly nothing is more material than a stone or a piece of metal, and yet water, fire, air are also material, but less solid than a stone or piece of metal. They are also higher in nature and are of greater value. The same is true of light and radiation which are even less material but no less real. When we consider the life-principle in plants and animals we encounter something far removed from the materiality of a stone, but also something that is very real and more perfect. Thus we see that as things become less material and sensible they increase in their perfection and value.

When we consider man, the highest creature in our visible world, we find that what makes him superior to all other creatures are his rational powers of intellect and will. It is these powers in man that are responsible for the vast difference that exists between a jungle and a modern city. But these two faculties are spiritual. Our intellect forms universal ideas like kindness, relationship and sin. These have no size, color, shape, weight or sound, none of the qualities of matter, yet they are very real. Hence these faculties and the soul in which they reside must be spiritual for they embrace realities that have nothing material about them.

That our intellect is a spiritual power is also evident in its ability to reflect back on what it has done before. The animal can know, but it cannot know that it knows, for it cannot reflect back on its act of knowing. If you could not think, what would it be like? You could see, hear, feel, but you could not reflect on what these meant nor could you freely decide on what to do by reason of those perceptions, for you would be determined by instinct. That is why the will, which is also a spiritual faculty, always accompanies the intellect. By it we can freely choose what to do with regard to the knowledge our intellect gives us. In the will alone is found the free act of love: the act of choosing a good.

Knowledge and love are spiritual realities and by them man is seen as being far superior to the whole material creation. That knowledge and love are spiritual is also obvious from the fact that we do not become physically heavier as we increase in knowledge and love. Then too, unlike material things, which cannot be wholly possessed by several persons at the same time, spiritual realities can be possessed by many persons, without any limitation to the number of persons possessing such knowledge and love.

But just what is a spiritual reality? We can only visualize a spirit as a power: something that is invisible, and yet it can produce a real effect.

Knowledge and love the only spiritual realities: We only know of two spiritual realities: knowledge and love, and these, as such, always exist in a person, in God, in man and in angels. Knowledge and love make up the very being, life and activity of a spiritual nature or person.

Some evolutionists, seeing the marvelous intelligence displayed in the universe are postulating a Cosmic Mind. They fail to realize that in doing so they are really postulating God, for intelligence can only exist in a person.

Another aspect of spiritual realities: knowledge and love, is that they are the only things that have lasting value. All material things will pass away for us at death, but our knowledge and love will go on with us into the future life. That is why many, who have had a near-death experience, testify that they were given to see that knowledge and love are the only things that really matter in this life and for eternity.

Some people do not wish to admit that these near-death experiences prove there is an after-life. However, they do prove that man's knowledge does not depend on his body, for many, having a near-death experience, found themselves very conscious while existing apart from their bodies and even looking down on them. Hence, these experiences certainly prove that man's intellectual life can exist apart from his body and that therefore an after-life is possible and also very likely.

B) WHY GOD CREATED

God exists and he is the first cause of everything else that exists. But why did God create? If we are to know ourselves and our true goal in life, we must know why and for what end God made us. Every intelligent person always has a reason for whatever he does. So true is this that even when we kill time it is for the reason that we have nothing better to do at the moment. Since God is evidently supremely intelligent, he had to have a reason for his great work of creation.

Until we know that reason we will have very little chance of understanding God's way of dealing with man. We may not be able to know the fullness of his reason for, "Who has known the mind of God?" (Rom. 11: 34) But we can and should be able to know something of his reason by considering the nature of things he has made and still more from what he has told us in his divine revelation.

God created to give: An intelligent person only acts out of love for some good and this is true of God himself. Since God alone existed before he created, he had to act out of love for himself. However, being infinitely perfect and lacking nothing, he could not act out of love for himself by seeking some additional good as is generally true of ourselves. His only reason had to be in order to manifest his glory and goodness by giving and sharing of his abundance with others. St. Thomas Aquinas says, "It belongs to imperfect agents to act in order to acquire something, for they still lack their full perfection, but this does not befit God, and therefore, he is supremely liberal because he acts, not for his utility, but only because of his goodness." (Sum. I, 44, 4 ad 1)

We may find it difficult to understand how one can act out of love for himself by giving, but even we can do the same through the love of benevolence. In the love of benevolence one seeks another person's good more than his own. A mother will spend herself for her family just for the joy of making others happy. A professor can find a real joy in sharing his knowledge with others that they too may profit from it. The reason why we can act in this way is that, when we love ourselves perfectly, we not only will what is good to us, such as to exist, to know, to be happy, but also what it is good for us to do, namely, to share our gifts with others. So parents find joy in sharing with their children. Indeed, a person can find greater joy in sharing his gifts than in obtaining additional gifts for, as Jesus tells us, "It is a more blessed thing to give than to receive." (Acts 20:35)

The measure of one's giving: Being absolutely perfect, God can only act out of love for himself by giving, and, being infinite in goodness, his giving will be beyond anything we might imagine possible. The measure of one's giving depends on *two things*: on the greatness of the gift he has to give and his own love for it, and on the goodness or love he has for himself which moves him to do what it is good for him to do. When we apply these two criteria to God we can begin to see something of the vastness of his love and his desire to share his gifts with us. The good which God possesses and which he loves is his own infinite being and happiness, and his desire to do what is good for him to do is also infinite. What God, therefore, really wants to share with us is actually his own infinite being and happiness in so far as he can give and we are capable of receiving.

However, in his desire to share his happiness with us, God is not content just to fill us with his gifts, he wants us to know that still greater joy of giving and sharing in our turn. That is one reason why God made us free: so that, recognizing his gifts to us, we might be willing and happy to share them in our turn and so become perfect even as our Heavenly Father is perfect. Parents find joy in sharing with their children, but they also want their children to become good and generous so that they might know the joy of giving and becoming useful members of society. What a joy it is when parents see their child developing and excelling in all its endeavors. So it is that God rejoices when he sees us growing in holiness by becoming more perfect in giving and sharing.

God also wants us to know the joy of achieving, the joy of victory. If a baseball team were given the pennant at the end of the season, although they had not won a single game, they would see it more as an insult. But, if they had really worked hard and came out on top, that pennant would mean far more to them than its monetary value. That is what God wants heaven to be for us: a reward of victory, as he tells us in Revelation, "Those who prove victorious I will feed from the tree of life set in God's paradise." (Rev. 2:7) When God allows so many trials and sufferings to afflict us in this life, it is only that we might grow through them in charity, and thus obtain a higher degree of glory and happiness in heaven. God wants us to know, not only the joy of receiving, but the greater joy of giving.

C) MAN'S PLACE IN CREATION

Mary is a creature, a member of humankind just as we are. Hence, whatever pertains to man in general also pertains to Mary. To understand Mary's place in God's plan of creation we need to have a clear understanding of man himself: his nature, his relationship with the rest of creation and the unity he should have within himself and with others, but especially with God.

If we have a false idea of who and what we are, we will make some very serious mistakes that will have eternal consequences. Today everyone, especially in the advertising business, is trying to tell us what is good or bad for man, but few seem concerned enough to know what man really is, so as to know what befits his being or does not. If I do not know the nature of a car, I may think that water is good in the gas tank. Such ignorance is nothing compared to what many people today think is good for man.

1. Man's nature: Man is a combination of body and spirit. We know quite well what is good For man's body, but our real problem is in knowing what is good man's spiritual soul. In the book of Genesis God said, "Let us make man to our own image and likeness." (Gen. 1:26) This he has done by making man an intelligent being with the two faculties of intellect and free-will. By these two powers we have desire and the capacity to know and to be known, to love and to be loved, which evidently requires mutual relationships with other intellectual beings. That is why people are our greatest joy, even as they are our greatest sorrow when we lose them in death or in some other way. Upon reflection we can see that there is nothing we desire more than to know and to be known, to love and be loved. And because we have the capacity to know all truth and to love all goodness, we want to be united, in mutual knowledge and love with someone who is all truth and goodness, namely, God. That is why God has to be our final goal if we want to find perfect happiness and fulfillment. Man is essentially a social being: he is incomplete in his nature without another person, another self or co-relation.

This is also true of God to whose image and likeness we have been made. Plato is said to have asked, "If God exist, whom does he know, whom does he love?" This is the closest human reason has ever come to suspecting the Trinity. Plato saw that no intelligent being can exist in isolation, that such a one needs to find his happiness and fulfillment in a mutual knowing and loving with another person. Through revelation we find that this is true of God himself in the mystery of the Trinity: God is one in nature and being, but three in persons, all united in mutual knowledge and love.

We cannot fully know how three persons can exist in one nature, but we can offer some understanding of its possibility. In the Trinity, the Father having the fullness of all being, knows himself and this knowledge has to be as perfect and infinite as God himself, and hence, it is himself but as another person, his Son, who is equal to the Father in every way. The Father and the Son, seeing each other to be so perfect, love one another and this love has to be as perfect and infinite as God himself and hence it is himself, but as another person, the Holy Spirit, the mutual love of Father and Son. Because God is one in nature, but a plurality of persons, he is the source, not only of all individuality, but also of everything social.

When God made the first man, Adam, he said, "It is not good for man to be alone" and so he gave him Eve as a helpmate. Since the creature cannot be as perfect as God, Adam, by knowing himself, could not produce another person, another self equal to himself. That is why God created Eve as Adam's other self. That too is why God willed that Adam and Eve should unite in mutual knowledge and love and, through marriage, be fruitful of a child, thus completing their likeness to God in his Trinitarian life. Marriage or the social unit of the family, is the most perfect and essential natural good and goal of mankind.

2. Man as a social unity: Man is essentially a social being who finds his most natural fulfillment in the family. However, God willed that mankind should be made up of many families or persons forming a larger social unit. These larger social units are formed according to the will and choice of man himself, but they are intended by God as part of his plan for creation. Therefore, they possess certain rights and duties derived from God himself. While there are smaller social groups, as clubs, churches, organizations and the like, it is the civil society of the state that has a special value for man as a social being. A family is not wholly sufficient in itself. It needs other people in many ways. We need doctors, layers, policemen, firemen, many different trades of workmen, the military and politicians. Only in the larger civil society can these various social needs be fulfilled. That is why the civil state is said to be the perfect society, since it covers all of man's many needs, at least in the physical order.

Civil society contains many blessings for mankind. With regard to mutual friendship, it unites us in love and service with many other people, thus enlarging our field of joy and happiness to be found in one another. It gives us the capacity to do many great works the individual or the family could never achieve: great building projects, scientific discoveries, space exploration and even war for mutual protection. The civil state can and should tend to unite its subjects in true brotherly love so that all share in the talents and even the personalities of all other citizens. Man is not made to live only for himself in a selfish way. He is part of the human family that finds its perfection, fulfillment, and happiness in mutual relationships with all the members of the human race. That is the natural goal God has intended for mankind, but, because of human pride and selfishness, that goal will never be perfectly achieved among us in this world.

The society of the civil state has certain needs which entail duties on the part of the members of society. Every society needs a leader to guide the group to its common goal for which they have freely united. That goal will differ according to the different reasons for which the society was established. But for the civil state that goal is recognized as being the common good of all its members. Although for the state that common goal is limited to the physical and material well-being of its members, it should not obstruct their higher spiritual needs, that is, their religious aspirations.

The choosing of a leader, even for the civil state, rests with the free choice of its members. They are free to choose or accept any form of government, monarchy, oligarchy or democracy. However, the authority of a legitimately chosen leader is derived from God who has willed the institution of the civil state. Therefore, the citizens have a moral obligation to obey such chosen leaders so long as they act within their authority and order nothing contrary to God's higher law. Since the leader and the government serve the common good, all the citizens are obliged to support them and the works they promote for the common good, by paying taxes. Since the leader acts in the name of all, the citizens are affected by the decisions he makes. This is very evident when he makes a declaration of war. As we shall see this also has its application with regard to the whole human race before God.

The bond of unity in social groups: When several individuals agree to work together they need some common bond of unity over and above that given by the leader. That bond of unity for the family and the civil state will be either charity or justice. Certainly mutual love or charity should be the bond that unites a family. If it does not, then there is something very wanting in that family. In other social groups love or charity is also the highest and best bond, but due to human selfishness it is not sufficient for larger social groups, especially the civil state, where justice is the only workable bond. It is justice that states that when one does a service for another he receives a patent for his work or an item of exchange and that, in this way, no one can take advantage of the other so long as justice is observed. This explains why communism will never work in the civil state. To expect a larger social group to hold everything in common, and to have each one, while working to his full capacity, willing to receive from the common source only according to his needs, requires a selflessness that men in general simply do not possess. Such a way of life is only possible in certain religious groups where the love of God is strong enough to overrule man's innate selfishness.

What is love and charity: I will be speaking often of love and charity, so it will be good to make clear what I mean by these terms. Charity is a special form of love. Love is the source of the joy and fulfillment one experiences in either having or receiving a good: (the love of concupiscence) or in giving and sharing a good with others (the love of benevolence). The higher act of love is not found in receiving, for this befits only imperfect agents, but in the act of giving, which is most perfect in God who can only act by giving and sharing. Thus the joy of loving is not found so much in having and receiving as in the act of giving and sharing or in using the gifts we have received. If I have eyes but never open them I cannot know the joy of seeing. So it is with all God's gifts, we really possess them only by using and sharing them. Remember, the servant who buried his talent, had it taken away from him. (Mt. 25:28) He never really made it his own by using and giving it.

Although we often use the terms love and charity as synonymous there is a real distinction between them. Love can be used for the love of concupiscence and the love of benevolence, but charity, strictly, applies only to the love of benevolence, a love that finds its joy in doing good, in making others happy.

We should note that, as St Thomas Aquinas says, charity does not increase by additional acts, but rather by an act more intense than any that went before it. Repeated acts may help to dispose one for a more intense act, but charity grows only when one performs a more intense act. For example, during the day I may be doing my normal tasks out of love for God and then there arises a trial that demands a much greater sacrifice of myself in order to please God. If I prefer to please God by sacrificing myself, my act becomes more intense and so my charity is increased. The greater the demand and the greater the sacrifice of self required in order to prove my love for God, the greater my charity becomes. Therefore, to sacrifice one's life out of love for God is seen as the highest act of charity, according to those words of our Lord, "Greater love than this no man has that he should lay down his life for his friend. (Jn. 15:13)

3. Man as king and mediator of creation: Since man has been made to the image and likeness of God, he is the highest of God's visible creatures and also the only one capable of knowing creation and God himself. Hence, he is both the king of creation and also its mediator with God. Without man creation would have no purpose or value for it would then be known only by God. But God has no need of such knowledge for he knows in himself, far more perfectly, all that creation contains.

Man as king of creation: Man is king of creation in a number of ways. First as being the highest of all God's visible creatures, so that all the rest of creation has been made to serve man. But man, in his turn, has been made for God: to know, love and serve God so as to find his happiness in God. Man, therefore has been given dominion over all creation that he might subdue it and use it for his own well-being and growth; not as its owner, but as its steward or administrator in the service of God, his loving master and friend. Thus man has the right to use freely all other creatures to serve his bodily needs, such as food, clothing, shelter and the like.

As for his rational life, man finds in creatures the source of all his natural knowledge. He abstracts from the sensible things his senses perceive, those universal concepts which make up the store of his knowledge. In this way, through creation, man also comes to know God. By seeing the wisdom, power and beauty manifest in creation, man comes to know of God's existence and his nature: that God is the supreme being upon whom he is utterly dependent.

Man as mediator of creation: Because of his social nature, once man comes to recognize who God is, he is drawn to seek some kind of friendly relationship with God. He does this through worship and, in so doing, he becomes the mediator bringing creation back to God in himself.

God is a perfect unity in himself, in his Trinitarian life, and everything God makes is stamped with unity. We find it in the universe as a whole where all the stars and galaxies are held together in one orderly cosmos through the forces of nature. We find it on our earth, in what is known as the balance of nature, which ecology tries to keep man from disrupting. We also find it in all living being which possess a wonderful unity in themselves. Therefore, just as everything came forth from God, so he has willed that everything should find its final perfection and fulfillment in coming back into unity with God in order that, in the end, God might be all in all.

Because God is a pure spirit, the material creation cannot be united directly to God but only through someone who is both spirit and matter, namely, man. Man therefore is the mediator whereby the material creation is capable of being united with God. For this man is most suited for a number of reasons. First because he is a kind of microcosm of creation containing in himself what are known as the four kingdoms of creation, in his body: the mineral kingdom, the vegetable kingdom and the animal kingdom, and in his soul: the rational kingdom. When therefore man unites himself with God in loving worship he brings all creation back to God in himself. Indeed, man actually employs the material creation in his very act of worship: praising God with song and musical instruments, offering victims in sacrifice to express his own total dependence on God and by using flowers, incense, candles, and the like to beautify and enhance the expression of his love for God.

Of course man is not a fully-adequate mediator of creation for, although man is perfectly united with the material creation, he is not perfectly united with God who is infinitely greater than man himself. Hence, for a perfect mediator we need a God-man, that is,

Jesus Christ, who, as we shall see when we come to consider the supernatural order of creation, can take man himself and all creation into unity with God in a fully perfect way. Christ, then, is the perfect mediator, uniting all mankind to God and, in man, all the material creation as well.

4. Man as a bond of unity: While man can unite the material creation with God, we must also know that man himself is a unity in his nature and on three different levels: in his individual nature, in his social nature and as a human race.

Man a unity in his individual nature: As an individual, man is made up of matter and spirit, body and soul. It is as though God took a piece of mud and a ray of light and made them into a fully integrated reality. So close is the unity between man's body and soul that, according to scholastic philosophy, when man's soul is separated from his body he is no longer a person in a strict sense. A person is defined as, a complete intellectual nature, but man is not complete in nature without his body and hence, in a strict sense, he is not a person.

Because Greek and scholastic philosophy recognize a clear distinction between man's body and soul, whereas the Jews in the Bible always speak of them as a single reality, some people are very critical of Greek and scholastic philosophy. Such criticism is without foundation. It is Hindu philosophy, with its idea of reincarnation, that really separates man from his body, making it something merely accidental. While it is true that the Bible generally speaks of man as an integral whole, it also recognizes a distinction between man's body and soul. This is very evident in Ezekiel's vision of the dry bones. When the bones were clothed with flesh they did not come to life until the breath of the spirit came into them.

In his individual nature man also is or should be a unity of life. In man there are actually three principles of life: the sensitive or animal life of his body, the intellectual life of his soul and, through the supernatural gift of grace, God's own divine life, as we shall see later. All of these should work together in perfect harmony. When several lives are united in some way the lower life should always be subordinate to the higher, as a horse to its rider, otherwise there will be trouble for the higher life. In man then, a twofold subordination is required. His sensitive life must be submissive to his rational life and his rational life must be submissive to God's higher divine life through faith.

If man lets his sensitive life dominate his reason, he degrades himself, as seen in the drunkard and the sex pervert. In his original creation God, by a special gift, made man's sensitive life to be perfectly submissive to man's reason and will, but this was lost through the sin of our first parents. Now man has to labor to bring his sensitive life into submission to his reason and will. Only by achieving such a subordination can man become a truly free and well-integrated person who is master of himself and not a slave to his passions.

Moreover, if man is to live the still higher divine Life of God he must bring both his sensitive life and his rational life into submission to God's divine life and will through faith, somewhat as a horse by submitting to the guidance of its rider can share in man's rational life even though it has no knowledge of doing so. Hence, when man is submissive to God's will through faith, God can do divine works through man and in this way man has a part in the fulfillment of God's divine plan for creation.

Man a unity in his social nature: We have already seen that man is essentially a social being who must find his happiness and fulfillment in a union of mutual knowledge and love with other intelligent beings. This he normally finds first in the family and then in the larger society of the civil state.

In the human family husband and wife and children should all be united in the love of benevolence so that they seek their happiness more in the happiness of the other than in their own happiness. If selfishness begins to predominate among them, their unity will suffer and will eventually lead to divorce.

But man also needs the larger society of the civil state. Here again all should live together in a unity of mutual sharing through charity or justice so as to promote the common good of all.

Both of these social unities flow from man's very nature which he cannot change. Now for every nature there are some things that are good and others that are not. Thus for the man-made nature of the car, some things are good and others are not. That is why car owners are given a manual to guide them on how to care for their car. In somewhat the same way God has given man a manual to guide him in what is good for his social nature. This manual is the natural law: the decalogue or ten commandments. It is found primarily in man's conscience, that is, in those spontaneous judgments of his reason, telling him what he should or should not do. Animals are guided in what is good for their nature by instinct, but man, being free, is guided to what is good for his nature by these spontaneous judgments of his reason, which he is free to follow or not. When he follows them he finds peace, when he does not he experiences guilt.

Since man's social well-being and happiness consist in living a life of mutual knowledge and love with other persons, his conscience simply tells him what is good or bad for such a life, both with God and with his fellow men and women. Thus we find that the first three precepts of the decalogue deal with man's proper relationship with God and the last seven with his proper relationship with his fellow men and women.

As for God, man must acknowledge the true God and not turn to false ones. He must honor God's name and take time from his daily tasks to worship God as his creator and benefactor.

With regard to his fellow men and women there is first of all the mutual love of family. Hence children must obey their parents and parents must take due care of their children. The greatest evil against the mutual love we owe another is to take his life and the next is to disrupt his family by adultery. Stealing is contrary to the right of another to keep the material goods he has won, and lying destroys the mutual confidence necessary for good relationships with others. Because the desire for possessions and the pleasure of sex are the greatest sources of human selfishness, we are forbidden to covet these things, that is, to seek them inordinately. All of these points are contained in the last seven precepts of the decalogue and pertain to our relationships with our fellowmen. They can be summed up in the golden rule: "Do unto others as you would want them to do unto you." Also all the precepts pertaining both to our relationships with God and with one another are summed up in the two great commandments of the law: love of God and neighbor.

As one can see, the morality of the decalogue is not based on any particular religion, but on man's very nature and therefore, it is basic to the well-being of every society regardless of its religion. If we do not believe that man's well-being depends on the observance of the decalogue, just look at the world around you today, and you will see that all its evils (other than natural disasters) flow from the fact that the precepts of the decalogue are not observed.

Man a unity as a race: Man has a still broader unity than that of the family and civil state: the unity of the human race itself. Every man or woman is a unique personality with gifts no one else has in the same way. Therefore, if we are to know and possess the fullness of our humanity, we must be united in mutual knowledge and love with every other human being. Of course that is impossible in our present life, but it does indicate what is necessary so as to enjoy the full possession and perfection of our humanity.

Some Father's of the Church have seen this unity of the human race as symbolized in two of our Lord's parables: the lost sheep and the lost drachma. (Lk. 15) The ninety-nine sheep that did not stray, they saw as the nine choirs of angels, while mankind was the one sheep that Jesus went in search to find. In the parable of the woman who had ten drachma, the nine were the nine choir of angels and mankind the one she lost and set out to find.

Mankind is indeed a single race and when we come to consider God's supernatural plan we will find that God has willed to deal with mankind as such. When Adam as the first head of the human race sinned, he lost God's offer of friendship for the whole race of mankind, but when Jesus as the new head of regenerated mankind won our salvation, he restored God's offer of divine friendship to the whole human race.

CHAPTER II

MARY IN THE SUPERNATURAL ORDER OF CREATION

When we come to the supernatural order we enter into the world of God and his divine revelation. We can have no knowledge of God's own inner life and will except through what he tells us. And since God cannot be ignorant or intend to deceive us, what he tells us must be absolutely true even if above our understanding. On our part, however, we must be careful to discern whether what is said to be from God really is so. There are a number of claims to divine revelations that do not agree and so cannot all be from God. Then too, once we are certain that a revelation is truly from God, we must see that we understand its message correctly. Here is not the place to prove God's true revelation, but I wish to state that the one I consider to be true and the one I will treat is the Judeo-Christian revelation as found in the Bible. I also hold that this revelation can be correctly understood only through the Magisterium of the Roman Church, founded on Peter. Through Peter Jesus promised to preserve his Church from error to the end of time. (cf. Mt. 16:18)

Through creation our human reason can know that God created only to give and share of his abundance, but how he has willed to do that and to what extent, we only know through his divine revelation. There we find that he has willed to call all mankind to a personal union of friendship with himself in his divine life. And he has willed to accomplish this through a twofold plan, one which was conditional and second that is definitive. In the conditional plan he foresaw and allowed the first man, Adam, with his social partner Eve, as the natural head of the human race, to refuse his offer of friendship and so lose it for all mankind. But in his second definitive plan, he willed, through the Incarnation of his own Divine Son, as the new Adam, together with Mary as his new Eve, to redeem mankind from the sin of that first refusal and to renew his offer of friendship to mankind.

I will divide this chapter into four parts. In the **first** I will consider God's divine election, his conditional plan, its failure, and why he allowed it to fail. I will also consider the promise of his definitive plan. In the **second** part I will consider the preparation that preceded the fulfillment of his definitive plan both in the Old Testament and in the New Testament. In the **third**, I will treat of the fulfillment of his plan in the working of our redemption. In the **fourth**, I will consider its acceptance by God as evidenced in Christ's Resurrection and Ascension. In all four of these we will be especially interested in seeing the place Mary has in this work of our redemption.

A) THE DIVINE ELECTION

Because God is the eternal, total and the all-knowing being, all actual and possible reality is fully present to his knowledge and completely under the control of his will. Because of that, nothing can thwart God's final and definitive plan, not even man's free-will. But God can choose to let man's free-will thwart his conditional plan, since it is only a means to make his definitive plan more perfect. Nothing can exist or act without God, and therefore he knows in himself what every creature will do, even every free creature, in every possible circumstance. He does not have to wait to know how his free creatures will act before he can make his plans, for he knows all that in himself from eternity. That is why God can finalize his plan from eternity: his so called predestination. How God can know all this in himself, without hindrance to man's perfect freedom, we cannot know any more than we can know how God can always exist.

1. Christ at the center of God's plan: In Scripture God's plan for creation is nowhere more clearly expressed than in St. Paul's letter to the Ephesians. "Before the world was made he chose us, chose us in Christ to be holy and spotless and to live through love in his presence, determining that we should become his adopted sons through Jesus Christ." (Eph. 1:4-5) "He has let us know the mystery of his purpose, the hidden plan he so kindly made in Christ from the beginning to act upon when the times had run their course to the end, that he would bring everything together under Christ as head, everything in the heavens and everything on the earth and it is in him that we are claimed as God's own." (Eph. 1:9-11) Here we see that it is in and through Jesus as our mediator with God that we and all creation are called to be united with God in a life of holiness and purity, living in his presence a life of loving friendship as his adopted sons in Jesus Christ his eternal Son.

Christ is at the center of God's plan for creation, Mary is inseparably united with him as his other self, the new Eve. Indeed, she is contained in the one and same decree, as Pius IX states in his decree defining the Immaculate Conception of Mary: "God the Father predestined Jesus to natural Divine Sonship and Mary to be the mother of his Divine Son in one and the same divine decree." In decreeing that Christ should become man, God had to decree that he should be fully man as a social being and hence as united with his other self, Mary, even as Adam, was only complete as man with Eve. Just as all human beings are incomplete without a social relationship with another person, so when Jesus became man, he too was incomplete in his human nature without his other self. But his other self, as man, is really all mankind, his Mystical Body, the Church, which St. Paul calls the bride of Christ. But for Jesus, in his individual and mortal life on earth, his spouse or other self as man was Mary. Mary therefore, was decreed not only to be the mother of Jesus from whom he received his humanity, but also to be his spouse and other self who would be associated with him in his work of our salvation, just as Eve was associated with Adam in the fall.

In his divine election God also willed to deal with man as a single race. Man is a social being, not only in his individual nature, but as a member of a larger civil society and even as a race. It is as one united human race that God has willed to deal with mankind.

This becomes very evident in the fall of the first man as recounted in Genesis and in the unfolding of God's great work of redemption as found in the New Testament.

In Genesis we find that through Adam's sin, as head of the human race, all mankind lost God's gift of grace and divine friendship and was plunged into a state of disgrace and debt before God. But Christ, becoming a new head of mankind, redeemed the whole human race from its former sin. Hence those words of John the Baptist, "Behold the lamb of God, behold him who takes away the sin of the world." (Jn. 1:29) Paul saw this very clearly when he writes, "Just as all men died in Adam so all men will be brought to life in Christ." (1 Cor. 15:22) And again, "Adam prefigured the one to come...and...if it is certain that death reigned over everyone as a consequence of one man's sin it is even more certain that one man Jesus Christ will cause everyone to reign in life who receives the free gift he does not deserve of being made righteous." (Rom. 5:15-17)

What follows from this is that, just as Adam was complete as man with Eve in our fall, so Jesus is to be complete as man with Mary in our restoration to God's grace and favor. Many Fathers of the Church, seeing Christ as the new Adam, also saw Mary as the new Eve. In the divine election, then, Mary is inseparable from Jesus, not only as being his mother but also as being his spouse and bride, acting as such with Jesus in the name of all mankind.

2. God's first conditional plan: God's first conditional plan is found in the account of man's creation in the book of Genesis. There we see God offering himself in intimacy to Adam and Eve, by walking with them in the cool of the evening, an obvious gesture of friendship. (Gen. 3:8) But friendship is something we must freely accept for it cannot be forced upon us. Therefore, God willed to test our first parents to see if they truly preferred his offer of friendship. And so he gave the command not to eat of the tree of life. At the suggestion of Satan, however, our first parents were persuaded to doubt God's good will towards them. Then, through pride and the desire for independence, he moved them to disobey God's command, thus refusing God's offer of friendship. In this test they were acting as the natural head and leader of the whole human race and so they lost God's offer of friendship, not only for themselves, but for all their posterity, much as when the head of a family loses the favor of the king, his whole household suffers with him.

In punishment for this sin God took away from man the so-called preternatural gifts which he had given man, over and above the requirements of his nature, in view of man's call to his divine friendship. By these gifts man's bodily desires were fully subject to the higher life of man's will. But when he lost them, his body became subject to death and his bodily desires were no longer perfectly subject to the higher aspirations of his spirit. Also, by breaking his bond of unity with God, the rest of creation was no longer perfectly subject to man: animals became wild and the earth more productive of weeds than of crops.

This sin of our first parents is known as original sin, and it is clearly different from all personal sins. It is a sin of our nature, a kind of spiritual and moral genetic defect that is inherited by all those who are born into the human race. Mersch, in his book *The Theology of the Mystical Body*, sees the essence of original sin as consisting in the fact that, since God has not withdrawn his offer of friendship, man exist in a state of rejecting that friendship with no possible remedy within himself. Because of original sin man exists in a state of opposition to God's will, and can do nothing to change it.

One may ask, "How much truth is there in the story of Adam and Eve?" While much of it may be symbolic as presented in Genesis, it does contain defined truth on at least four counts.

1. The first couple, of our present human race, were created with original justice.
2. Through sin they lost that gift of original justice for themselves and for the whole human race.
3. Christ by his redemption has made satisfaction for original sin and all sin.
4. Individuals receive the effects of Christ's redemption by receiving baptism.

Why God permitted the fall: Another question we may ask is, "Why did God permit the fall of our first parents?" Certainly one reason was they he might reveal his merciful goodness in a more ineffable way so as to inspire man to the highest possible degree of charity in a return of love. There is nothing exceptional in being good to one who has been good to us, but to be good to those who have offended and who hate us is to be good to an heroic degree. The fall gave God a chance to reveal his love in a way that is so divine that we are overwhelmed by it.

God willed to send his own divine Son to become man and to suffer the penalty of our sin committed against himself, that we, the sinners, might go free. Nothing can move us more to love God in return than the sight of such great love. Indeed, if God had not so loved us to an infinite degree, would the martyrs and the saints have been moved to their heroic love for God in return? Nothing can move us to accept God's offer of friendship more than the extravagance of God's own love for us.

The fall had other good effects also. It gave God a chance to prove the lie of Satan, who had represented God as being selfish and jealous of his prerogatives. How can man now think of God as being selfish when he has chosen to die in our place and what a death.

Even the punishment meted out to man, because of his sin, was to prove a blessing. Man sinned because of pride, wanting to find his well-being in himself. But now, with the loss of the preternatural gifts, he has such an experience of his weakness and misery that he has little grounds for pride. I like to think that God foresaw from the beginning that our present fallen state, with all its misery, was by far the best for us, so as to save us from the mortal danger of pride. But had he created us in that imperfect state, we would have gravely questioned his goodness. Now that we have fallen into it by our own fault we can only blame ourselves and not God.

Another blessing occasioned by the fall is that we now have as the head and ruler of our human race, not a mere man, but God himself in his divine Son Jesus of whom Adam was only a figure. The Church recognizes this and, seeing how much more we have received in Jesus than we lost in Adam, has been moved to sing in her Exulte [at the Easter Vigil,] "O happy fault that has won for us so great and marvelous a redeemer."

3. The promise of God's definitive plan: Immediately after the fall, God promised mankind a savior, thus indicating his second and definitive plan for mankind. We find it revealed very subtly in the third chapter of Genesis. Speaking to the Devil who tempted Eve, God said, "I will make you enemies of each other: you and the woman, your offspring and her offspring. It will crush your head and you will strike its heel." (Gen. 3:15) Here we see that the woman and her offspring will be set against the devil and his offspring and that her offspring will prevail but not without suffering from the offspring of Satan. God's salvation will come through the offspring of Mary, that is, through Jesus Christ her son, with whom she will be united as Eve was united with Adam as his spouse.

God could have chosen to redeem mankind in many other ways, in fact he could have simply pardoned man, once man had repented and asked forgiveness. However, any other way would not have been as effective and glorious for God and as honorable for man. God, therefore, willed to save mankind from within itself by giving mankind the means whereby to redeem itself through one of its own members. He chose to send his divine Son to become a member of our human race so that, being man and having the dignity of God he could make adequate reparation for mankind's offense against God. How he has willed to bring this, his definitive plan, to its perfect fulfillment, we will now consider, but let us first consider its preparation in both the Old Testament and New Testament.

B) THE PREPARATION OF GOD'S DEFINITIVE PLAN

The fulfillment of God's definitive plan for mankind's salvation is generally divided into what is known as the Old Testament and the New Testament. In the Old Testament it consisted in the preparation of a particular people in whom the coming Messiah would find the proper circumstances for the fulfillment of his mission. In the New Testament, wherein we find the accomplishment of that redemption, there is also a period of preparation before the actual work of our redemption.

1. Preparation in the Old Testament: Here there are three things we must consider. First of all, man's redemption was not immediate. Then there was the preparation of a chosen people and finally the special preparation of Mary who was to have a central and essential role in the work of our salvation.

a. Redemption was not immediate: God did not send the Messiah, the savior, immediately after the fall. Looking back we can see some of the reasons for this. Man had sinned through pride, thinking he could provide for his own well-being without God. Hence God had to humble man's pride so that he might be ready to acknowledge his helplessness and be ready to accept God's new offer of friendship. But it would take time for man to come to a full experience of just how helpless he really is. That is why God left man to flounder in ignorance and misery for some 4000 years until he was convinced that he needed outside help and that he was not sufficient unto himself. The tragedies, the many religious searchings and the despair of people down the centuries bear witness to man's inability to solve his deepest spiritual and moral needs. Even today we see the misery, skepticism and despair of those who try to run their human lives without God.

Although God left mankind much to itself for so many centuries, still he did not want man to lose hope of his promised redemption. Therefore he chose to raise up a people through whom his promise of a future redeemer would be kept alive and through whom other people and nations would come to know of it. Not only would God seek to preserve a hope in his coming redemption, he also willed to train this people through a living experience of himself so that his future Messiah would find the proper conditions for the fulfillment of his mission.

b. The chosen people of God: God's preparation for his redemption started in the Old Testament with the call of Abraham some 2000 years before the coming of Jesus. God asked Abraham to leave his country and his father's house for a land he would show him. When he had obeyed, God made three promises to Abraham:

1. That he would make him into a great nation. (Gen. 12:2)
2. That he would give to his descendants the promised land. (Gen. 15:18)
3. That all the nations of the earth would be blessed in him. (Gen. 12:3)

That God should give these promises to Abraham and fulfill them hundreds of years, even thousands of years, later through actual historical events is the greatest proof of the divine origin of the Judeo-Christian revelation. No man could make promises that would be fulfilled after a span of hundreds and even thousands of years. And God did just that in ways Abraham could never have foreseen. Although he was childless at the time, God gave him Isaac in his old age who became the father of Jacob. It was Jacob or Israel who went into Egypt with his family and became a numerous people. Reduced to slavery by Pharaoh for 400 years, his people were delivered through Moses by a miraculous event that would be a symbol of God's future redemption of mankind from the slavery of Satan. Then, after training them for 40 years in the desert he led them into the land he had promised to Abraham where they became a nation set apart: united to God by a covenant.

However, they often proved unfaithful to God and were continually turning to the worship of alien gods so that God had to keep correcting them in various ways. When they proved incorrigible he destroyed them as a nation and sent them into exile for 70 years. Upon their repentance he brought back a remnant to their own land and from this remnant he formed a people fit and ready to receive his promised Messiah. In the midst of this renewed people he prepared various individuals who would have a direct and personal part in the fulfillment of his plan of redemption. Among these were John the Baptist and his parents Zachariah and Elizabeth. Then there were the parents of Mary, Joachim and Ann, and especially Mary herself along with Joseph. There were also the apostles and many other people who in the Gospel were to be associated with Jesus and the early Church in various ways.

As we shall see, the third promise made to Abraham, "That in him all the nations would be blessed," found its fulfillment only in Jesus and in the preaching of his salvation to all the nations at Pentecost. Its fulfillment was truly divine, for no writer of the Old Testament could have foreseen it in any human way.

c. The special preparation of Mary: Of all those individuals prepared by God in the Old Testament, Mary is the most outstanding, for she was to be the mother of the Messiah and associated with him in his work of redemption as the new Eve. For her exalted role she was given special graces and privileges of which three are most important.

The first is Mary's Divine Motherhood with the gift of her Immaculate Conception. In view of her Divine Motherhood, Mary, through the foreseen merits of Jesus, was preserved from all stain of original sin from the first moment of her conception and from all subsequent sin. While other faithful people in the Old Testament were given grace through the foreseen merits of Jesus, Mary alone shared in them by way of prevention. Hence, she was never under the stain of original sin.

That she should be so privileged was most fitting. She was to be united with Jesus, the God-man, as his mother and spouse. It was only right, then, that she should be spotless and holy. Any blemish in her would have reflected back on her divine Son. Then too, if someone were able to choose the one to be his mother (as God had the power to do) surely he would not choose one who was a former slave or enemy when he could choose one of queenly goodness. And if he could endow such a one with every possible beauty and gift, would he not do so? Also, since the Son of God came to take away sin, surely he would not choose a sinner for his mother. It is to the glory of a child to be born of noble parents. Hence, the Son of God would surely see that his own mother would be the most noble of all mothers. God, who had the power to bring Eve into the world immaculate, did not lack the power to make Mary to be born immaculate.

A second privilege of Mary is that she was also given the fullness of all grace. In the New Testament Jesus is said to be full of grace (Jn. 1:14) and Mary also (Lk. 1:30) However, they have this fullness in different ways. Jesus has the fullness of grace as the active principle of our salvation, Mary has the fullness of grace as its passive recipient. Whatever of grace can be received from Christ's redemption Mary has received in all its fullness, so that no other creature can possess a grace that is not first to be found in Mary. It is this fullness of grace that enabled Mary to correspond with absolute fidelity to the mission God had entrusted to her as the mother and spouse of Jesus. And because of her absolute fidelity Mary was never stained by any personal sin, a fact which is also proclaimed in the definition of her Immaculate Conception.

Knowing ourselves, we may readily ask, "How can a human being be so perfect as never to do anything that is not defective in some way?" Part of the answer to that question is that Mary was free from concupiscence: that result of the Fall whereby bodily passions are no longer perfectly subject to our rational will. However, the main answer seems to be, as someone has suggested, that Mary was possessed by the Holy Spirit. In diabolic possession the devil can fully dominate the bodily powers of a person, but not their will. Hence, they are able to refuse their consent to all the devil does through their bodily members. Of course the Holy Spirit, who is love personified, would never so dominate a person, but he would invite that person always to do the absolutely perfect thing in every circumstance of his daily life. Since Mary's will was always perfectly attuned by grace to wanting God's will, she never failed to heed that guidance of the Holy Spirit within her. It is difficult for us to visualize such absolute perfection, but it is said of St. John of the Cross that near the end of his life he appeared to be moved by the Holy Spirit in everything he did. If a saint could receive that grace at the end of his life, surely Mary could have received it from the very beginning of her life.

Another privilege that Mary received which is seldom stressed in an explicit way is Mary's motherliness. In God there is the fullness of every perfection including those perfections we know as masculine and feminine. When Jesus became man, however, he was limited by his male nature, to revealing only those perfections proper to the masculine nature. Therefore, God willed to reveal his feminine perfections in Mary. Mary completes God's revelation of himself in the Incarnation. Hence, while Jesus reveals God's masculine perfections, Mary reveals his feminine perfections.

In Mary we find the motherly qualities of the God-head in their highest possible human expression. In her is revealed the fullness of his motherliness so that she could be the most perfect of mothers, not only to his divine Son, but also to all mankind, to all the members of Christ's Mystical Body. No creature could share in the motherliness of God more fully than Mary. When we love Mary, God sees us as loving his own motherliness in her. Mary is all mother for that is what God made her to be. In her are found God's motherly qualities of tenderness, self-sacrifice, compassion, gentleness and forgiveness in the highest degree. If we want to find God as mother, we must look for him in Mary.

2. Preparation in the New Testament: The preparation of God's plan for redemption continues in the New Testament with those events that prepared Christ for his public life and for his saving death and resurrection. This preparation started with the birth of John the Baptist and includes the Annunciation, the birth of Jesus and his hidden life. Before considering these various events, let us first look at what we would judge to be necessary for Christ to save us as being a member of our human race.

a. What was necessary for Christ to be our savior: To save us from within Christ had to be truly man, born into our human family like every other human being, and at the same time bringing with him a new principle of life, God's own divine life of friendship, which man had lost through the sin of our first parents. In the birth of every human being there are two principles required: one active, the male seed, and the other passive, the female egg. In the case of Christ the active principle, the seed of a new life, God's own life of friendship, was supplied by the Holy Spirit, God's creative Love. The passive principle, the human ovum, was supplied by Mary, the chosen mother of the Messiah. It is only through Mary that Jesus is truly a member of our human race, and a descendent from Abraham and David.

That the Messiah should be truly man was necessary for other reasons. One: that we might be able to know and understand God's love for us in a human way and know how to return that love. God, therefore, willed to lower himself to our level of mentality, somewhat as a mother in dealing and speaking with her little child. Without the incarnation God would have remained so aloof from us that we could never have entered into any true friendship with him, for friendship requires a certain equality. Becoming man was a great condescension on God's part. As St. Paul says, "He did not cling to his equality with God but emptied himself to assume the condition of a slave." (Phil 2:6)

That Jesus should be truly man was also necessary in order that he might unite us in friendship with God. Friendship requires a certain equality, but between the creator and the creature there can be no question of any true equality. However, when Jesus became man we could then enter into a human friendship with him, and being God he could take us up with himself in his friendship with his Father. Christ is our true and only mediator with God and that is why Jesus could say, "No one comes to the Father except by me." (Jn. 14:6)

By reason of the Incarnation, we are called to a twofold friendship with Jesus, one with Jesus as man and the other with Jesus as God. All the members of Christ's Mystical Body, the Church, are called to a loving friendship with Jesus as man. But Mary alone fulfilled that role with absolute perfection during Jesus' mortal life, and she did so, in union with Jesus as the new leader and head of the human race, much as Eve was united with Adam in our fall. Mary therefore, is our perfect Mediatrix with Jesus as man, and Jesus is our perfect mediator with his Father, as God.

b. The Annunciation of Christ's coming: The fulfillment of the above requirements began with the coming of John the Baptist and the Annunciation by the angel Gabriel to Mary. All the longings and prayers of the patriarchs and prophets of old and especially those of Mary herself, finally moved God to initiate the final preparation for the work of salvation.

When the angel came to Mary, she soon realized the purpose of his coming. She was being asked to be the mother of the Messiah. Since God respects the freedom of his creatures, the coming of Christ was wholly dependent upon Mary's consent. That God foresaw that she would give that consent did not lessen the merit of her consent nor her right to our gratitude in giving Jesus to the world.

Mary had only one difficulty with the angel's message: what about her vow or determination to remain a virgin. Since St. Matthew tells us that Mary was betrothed to Joseph, the natural meaning of the angel's words would be that, once the marriage was consummated, she would conceive the promised child. Therefore, when Mary asked, "How can this be for I am a virgin?" (Lk. 1:34) it could only indicate that she had determined to remain a virgin and that she felt that God still approved of her resolve. When the angel explained that she would conceive by the power of the Holy Spirit and that the child would be known as the Son of God, her difficulty vanished and she gave her consent.

But what about Joseph's place in all this? If Mary had made a vow of perpetual virginity she would have had to confide this to Joseph before the arrangement of the betrothal. Indeed, it would appear, as some have held, that Joseph agreed to live with Mary in mutual virginity and that perhaps by a similar vow of virginity. God certainly prepared Joseph for the sublime mission he was to receive of being the spouse of Mary and the foster father of Jesus. Hence, he must have been given a degree of holiness and virtue greater than any other saint. If some young Christian saints, like St. Aloysius, was given a very high degree of purity, surely St. Joseph was not less enriched with grace. Hence, we must see Joseph as a young man, slightly older than Mary, filled with the Spirit of God and a holiness comparable, in many ways, to that of Mary herself.

Seeing Joseph in this light can help us to solve his problem concerning Mary's pregnancy. Joseph certainly learned about the angel's visit from Mary herself. Not to have shared such an important happening with her husband would not have been an act of virtue on her part. Joseph, as her future husband, had every right to know of it. His problem, then, did not stem from doubting Mary's purity, but from his own humility: "Who was he to barge into the life of one whom the Holy Spirit had chosen as his bride?" That is why he was considering to put Mary aside privately without any public scandal. But, if he really thought Mary was unfaithful, he could hardly be called a just man for not rather denouncing her.

This interpretation can even be read in the Gospel text if we omit a single comma in the angel's words, "Joseph, son of David, do not be afraid to take Mary home as your wife (omit comma here) because what is in her she has conceived by the Holy Spirit." (Mt. 1:20) It was because she had conceived by the Holy Spirit that he was in doubt as to God's will for him with regard to Mary. But once he was assured by the angel he fulfilled his God-given mission with the utmost fidelity.

c. The Visitation: In his message to Mary the angel Gabriel had informed her that her cousin Elizabeth, who had been barren, was now six months with child since nothing is impossible with God. In our relationship with God we have a twofold duty, first to accept God's gifts and will in our life, and then to be generous in fulfilling what his gifts and will may require of us. At the Annunciation we see Mary's perfect docility in accepting God's will, and here in the Visitation we see Mary's perfect generosity and cooperation in fulfilling his will and in sharing his gifts with others.

Her reason for visiting her cousin was certainly to congratulate Elizabeth on the wonderful favor God had granted her, but also to help her cousin in the special needs giving birth would require. Thus Mary is a perfect model for both the contemplative life in receiving God's gifts, and also of the apostolic life in giving and sharing her gifts with others.

The Visitation is often seen as a sign of Mary's right to the title: Mediatrix of all graces. Because of her perfect docility to God's will, God was able to bring many blessings to others, even without her knowledge. Thus, through her visit, Jesus sanctified John the Baptist in his mother's womb. He also filled Elizabeth with the Holy Spirit and gave her to know Mary's divine motherhood. When he moved Elizabeth to praise Mary for her faith this occasioned Mary to give expression to the sentiments of her heart in the beautiful words of her Magnificat. As God used Mary in bringing Jesus with his gifts to Elizabeth and to John the Baptist so many of the faithful hold that God has willed to bring all his gifts of grace to mankind through Mary as the Mediatrix of all graces.

d. The birth of Jesus: As the time came for Mary to bring forth Jesus into the world, divine providence began its hidden work. Caesar called for a census of his empire which required Mary and Joseph to travel to Bethlehem where, according to the prophets, the Messiah was to be born. This decree occasioned some uncertainties and difficulties for Mary and Joseph, but trusting in God's providential care they made the journey in faith. When they were unable to find a suitable place, God directed them to find lodging in a cave. There in poverty and solitude, the savior of the world was born, thus revealing God's preference for what is poor, weak and humble. By his divine providence God so arranged everything as to give us the beautiful feast of Christmas which so touches and moves the human heart.

The only ones who were to witness this stupendous event in the history of the world, besides Mary and Joseph, were poor and humble shepherds, and those seeking true wisdom, the Magi. Those who were taken up with the pursuits of this world were not disposed to recognize the ways of God.

Mary gave birth to Jesus without loss to her virginity; Jesus came forth from her womb as he was to come forth from the sealed tomb at his resurrection. From the time of the early Fathers of the Church, Mary has always been proclaimed a virgin, *"Before, In* and *After* childbirth." This is a defined dogma and tradition of the Church. Mary's immaculate purity and integrity is not limited to her soul but also embraces her body; she is wholly beautiful without spot of wrinkle or any kind. Belief in Mary's perpetual virginity is not based on any external witness but comes from the Church's understanding of scriptural texts under the guidance of the Holy Spirit.

After the birth of Jesus, Mary and Joseph, faithful to the Mosiac law, followed its ruling concerning the circumcision of Jesus. It was then that he received the name of Jesus, given him by the angel before his birth. They did the same with regard to the presentation of Jesus in the temple, their first born male child, and the purification of Mary. God used the occasion to fulfill the promise he had made to holy Simeon, that he would see the Savior of the world before he died. He used it also to let Mary know that her child was to be a sign of contradiction to the world and that her own heart would have to suffer. The prophetess Anna also shared in welcoming the Savior of mankind and announced it to all who were interested.

Apparently after all these events, Joseph and Mary settled down in Bethlehem since that is where the Magi found them, in a house and no longer in a stable. Knowing that the Messiah was to come from Bethlehem, Joseph may have felt that that is where he should now settle his little family. The flight into Egypt put an end to their stay and no doubt put an end to what rumors there were in the air concerning the birth of God's promised Messiah. If Jesus were two years old at the time of the flight into Egypt, their journey would have been less difficult for Joseph and Mary. On their return from Egypt Joseph apparently thought of settling again in Bethlehem, but feared to do so when he heard that Archelaus, the son of Herod, had succeeded his father. Warned in a dream he settled in Nazareth and it was there Jesus lived his hidden life.

e. The Hidden life: It was at Nazareth that Luke tells us, "Jesus grew up and matured in wisdom and in favor with God and man." (Lk. 2:52) This must have been the happiest period of Mary's life, and also of Jesus and Joseph. How Mary must have rejoiced in seeing Jesus grow and develop into a lovely boy and then into a young man. Their lives were poor and simple, but they lived together in mutual love and sharing; a happy family all united in the love and service of God. Joseph was certainly the best of husbands and fathers, doing all he could to provide for the material needs of the family. And Mary must have been the most loving and devoted wife and mother, seeking to bring joy and happiness to all. Her cooking and needle work must have been the best, considering their limited means. The seamless undergarment, woven in one part from top to helm, mentioned by St. John at the crucifixion, (Jn. 19:23) was surely the work of Mary's love and skillful hands. Mary and Joseph had the greatest influence in the education and development of Jesus' childhood. The Holy Family remains the ideal model for every Christian home.

The three day loss: Only one event during the period of the hidden life of Jesus has been recorded in the Gospel: the three day loss and finding of Jesus in the temple. St. Luke tells us that Joseph and Mary were faithful in going up to Jerusalem for the Passover feast each year, and surely Jesus went with them. When Jesus reached the age of twelve, the age when a Jewish boy become an adult and a full subject of the Mosaic Law, something changed in that yearly event. Jesus remained in Jerusalem without telling his parents. Only after three days of an agonizing search did they find him among the doctors of the law in the temple.

Why did Jesus do this? Apparently it was to remind his parents, now that he was an adult according to the law, that he had a higher mission in life which he must one day fulfill. But why did he not tell his parents beforehand? Because the lesson he wanted to teach them would have been less effective in that way. So it is in our own lives, Jesus sometimes does things that seem incomprehensible to us, the reason for which we may not come to understand until many years later.

When Mary asked Jesus why he had done this to them, he replied, "Did you not know that I must be about My Father's business." (Lk. 2:49) We are told that Mary did not understand the meaning of his words, but kept all these things stored up in her heart. Did Mary recall this event when she experienced that far more painful separation from Jesus: his three days in the tomb? The two events would seem to be related. Jesus wanted his parents to realize that one day he would have to depart to fulfill his own

God-given mission in life. So it is that parents must come to accept the fact that God has a special task for their children and that they must not stand in the way, especially when he calls them to a religious or priestly vocation.

The knowledge of Jesus as man: After the finding in the temple, St. Luke tells us that Jesus went back to Nazareth with his parents and was subject to their authority. Although he had come of age Jesus willed to continue to live under the authority of his parents until the day when it was his Father's will for him to begin his mission of salvation.

Since these were the years when Jesus grew to his full maturity, many have concerned themselves about the knowledge of Jesus. Today some scholars are so intent on stressing the humanity of Jesus that they seem to be forgetting his divinity. While the Incarnation is certainly a mystery which we will never fully understand, still the Church has defined certain realities of that Mystery which we must be careful not to deny. The Church tells us that there is only one person in Jesus, the second person of the Trinity, who is God, equal to the Father and the Holy Spirit. It also tells us that Jesus possesses two complete natures, one human and the other divine. Therefore, the person of Jesus possesses all the knowledge proper to his divine nature and all that is possible to his human nature. How much of his divine knowledge he shared with his human intellect, theologians are free to speculate so long as they do not overlook the unity of person in Jesus.

It is always the person who knows; whether I know through my senses or through my reason. So too in Jesus it is the divine person who knows, whether it be through his human nature or his divine nature. To say that Jesus did not know who he was, is like saying the Son of God does not know who he is. He may not have known this through his human reason, but he certainly knew it through his divine knowledge. How much of his divine knowledge did Jesus share with his human nature, we have no way of knowing. But if we consider how man shares the knowledge he receives from his senses with that of his reason, it would appear that, in practice, they are perfectly united.

There are some passages in Scripture which seem to show limitations in Christ's human knowledge, and these some scholars tend to stress. But there are many other passages which show no limitations in his knowledge, and these they seem to ignore completely. That Jesus sometimes showed surprise, need not imply that he had no foreknowledge of what would happen, but only no experiential knowledge. A woman may read what it is like to give birth to a child, but the actual experience will be something quite different. What Jesus knew as man is not so all important; what is important is how much he has loved us both as man and as God.

Mary's knowledge of Jesus: What about Mary's knowledge; did she know that Jesus was God? Mary was surely given a greater understanding of Scripture and of the things of God than any saint at the time. Mary certainly knew that Jesus was the Messiah, one greater than Moses or any of the prophets, but that the Messiah would be God himself is never clearly stated in the Old Testament nor can we find any grounds for it in Jewish tradition. For a Jew, ingrained with the idea that God is one and that he cannot be depicted by any created image, it would have been impossible to think of a man as being God. Neither is there any clear indication of the mystery of the Trinity in the Old Testament. Son of God and Spirit of God are terms used in the Old Testament, but never understood as another person in God. Mary, therefore, could not have known the divinity of Jesus except by some divine revelation, However, we have no evidence that she was given such a revelation, at least before the resurrection of Christ. If she had known that Jesus was truly God's Son, and hence the mystery of the Trinity, she would have understood Jesus' answer, "Did you not know that I must be about my Father's business?" Since we are clearly told that she did not, we must hold that Mary had no certain knowledge of Jesus' divinity. Mary had to live by faith much as we do and she spent her life growing in her knowledge of God and of Jesus himself. That is why we are told that "Mary treasured all these things pondering, them in her heart." (Lk. 2:19) Mary knew that Jesus was the Messiah, but who the Messiah really was in his person, She came to know only gradually as any mother comes to know her child.

Death of Joseph: After Jesus returned to Nazareth with his parents we no longer hear any mention of Joseph. It is generally believed, therefore, that he died before Jesus began his public ministry. This belief is confirmed by the lack of any mention of Joseph during Jesus' ministry and by the fact that when dying on the cross Jesus committed his mother to the care of his disciple John. If Joseph were still living, there should have been no need for John to assume Joseph's responsibility.

There are some fitting reasons why it was appropriate for Joseph to die around this time. Once Jesus was old enough to support Mary, Joseph's mission was now fulfilled. Then too, once Jesus became of age for marriage, people would have begun to wonder and spread rumors had he remained unmarried for long. Since he did not start his public life until he was thirty, far beyond the normal age for a Jewish boy to marry, such rumors could well have risen. However, being the only son of his widowed mother would have given him some excuse for delaying marriage and thus afford less cause for gossip.

C) REDEMPTION AND MARY'S PLACE THEREIN

God sent his Son into the world in order to redeem the world and give back to man the possibility of accepting God's offer of divine friendship. As Mary had an essential place in the Incarnation, freely consenting to be the mother of Jesus, so in his work of redemption she is to have an essential place with Jesus as his spouse. Hence, she will be united with Jesus in his supreme act of sacrifice on the cross, acting in our place as his bride and other self.

Before considering the actual work of Christ's redemption and Mary's place therein, I would like to first consider some requirements for Christ's redemption role to be effective. I will also treat of Christ's public life which was as a preparation leading to the supreme moment of his redeeming sacrifice.

1. Some requirements for redemption: It is a principle, stated by some of the Fathers of the Church, that whatever was not assumed by Christ, was not saved. If Christ did not have a human body, then our bodies were not saved. If he did not have a human soul, our souls were not saved. If Christ acted only as an individual man and not as a complete social human being, then man would not have been saved in his complete social nature.

Christ also had to be the head and leader of a new mankind, a man who possessed the divine life of God and could impart it to those who would be born into that new humanity. That is why St. Paul could say that mankind is a new creation: a man who now lives by the life of God. He is as a new species of mankind.

As the social head and leader of this new humanity, Jesus needed his other self, his new Eve. It is Mary who was given to him to be that new Eve. Therefore, just as Eve had a vital role with Adam in our fall, so Mary is to have a vital role with Jesus in our redemption. As Eve is the mother of all those who are born into the humanity of which Adam is the head and leader, so Mary is the mother of all those who are born into the new humanity of which Jesus is the head and leader.

Jesus, by becoming man, unites us in friendship with his Father much as the son of a king who marries a girl takes her up with himself into the life of the royal family. In our case however, the spouse Jesus has taken to himself, all mankind, is at enmity with his Father because of a former offense. Therefore, if Jesus is to introduce us, his spouse, into the divine family of God he must first free us from that enmity due to our former offense. But he cannot do that without our consent, that is, unless we repent of our former offense and accept Jesus' offer to make amends for our sin. It is Mary who gave that consent in our place on Calvary. There she was united with Jesus as his spouse in his role as head and leader of a new mankind.

2. The Public life of Jesus: The purpose of Christ's public life was to prepare mankind to recognize and accept God's offer of salvation. Hence the first need was that man should be led to repentance, to a change of heart. He must stop living for self and the world, and learn to live for the higher things of God's spiritual kingdom. Man also needed to be instructed as to the nature of God's kingdom: that it was not a material or political kingdom, but a spiritual kingdom within the heart of man himself. What was needed was not a revolt against Rome, but a repentance from sin and the living of a new life of friendship with God, based on Faith, Hope and Love. Another purpose of Christ's public life was for Jesus to instruct his apostles so that they could carry on his work of salvation through the establishment of his Church after his own Resurrection and Ascension into heaven.

Mary in the Public life of Jesus: Mary was to have no part in the public life of Jesus apart from perhaps initiating it at Cana and sharing in Christ's supreme sacrifice on the cross. Her role was to be in the inner life of the kingdom and not in its apostolic ministry.

How Jesus took his departure from Mary and how much he told her about his future work we have no direct information. Apparently Jesus took his mother to Capernaum to live there with some relatives. St. Matthew tells us, "After John the Baptist had been arrested Jesus went back to Galilee and, leaving Nazareth, settled in Capernaum." (Mt. 4:12-13) From then on this was called his own town. (Mt. 9:1) Apparently Jesus' separation from his mother was not complete at first. It was only after Cana and the arrest of John the Baptist that Jesus left his mother with some relatives in Capernaum. No doubt he often visited with her whenever his travels brought him back to that town. But Mary must have also received information from others while he was on the road.

Only twice does Mary appear in the public life of Jesus: the first time at Cana where it would appear she launched Jesus on his public life by moving him to work his first miracle. However, Jesus used the occasion to remind Mary that this was not yet his supreme hour when she would be united with him in his redeeming work of salvation. No doubt Jesus had told her that she would be with him in that hour. We know that when St. John uses the expression, "His hour" he always refers to Christ's supreme sacrifice on the cross. Therefore, when Jesus tells Mary at Cana, "My hour has not come," he is telling her that this is not the time when she will be united with him in the final fulfillment of his mission.

The only other occasion when Mary appears in the public life of Jesus is when, with some of her relatives, they ask to see Jesus while he is in the house speaking to his followers. Jesus uses the occasion to announce that more blessed are those who hear the word of God and keep it than the privilege of being a blood relation of his. Here Jesus is not depreciating his love and esteem for his mother. For no one has excelled Mary in hearing the word of God and keeping it. He is only indicating the superiority of the spiritual over the natural or human.

John the Baptist in the Public life of Jesus: In his public life, Jesus was preceded by the preaching of John the Baptist: the herald who was sent before Jesus to prepare the way and to point Christ out to his people. His task was to lead the people to repentance and to a turning away from temporal pursuits to the higher realities of the spirit. He came not to preach a political revolt, but repentance and a change of life. Indeed, the greatest obstacle Jesus himself was to encounter in his public life was that the people, and especially their leaders, expected a political warrior as the Messiah. That is why Jesus himself, at the beginning of his ministry, also preached repentance and a change of life. The people's expectations had to change if they were to accept him as the Messiah.

John the Baptist had the added task of inaugurating Jesus on his mission of salvation as the savior of the world by baptizing him: he who would take upon himself the sin of the world in order to reconcile mankind with God. Here Jesus is seen as the scapegoat, burdened with the sins of his people.

Once John had finished his task of baptizing Jesus and of pointing him out as the Messiah, he had nothing more to do and so he passed from the scene, so that Jesus might increase while he might decrease. Jesus, after his baptism then went into the desert and fasted for forty days to obtain the strength needed to fulfill his mission of destroying the power of sin and Satan in the world.

The works of Jesus' Public life: At first Jesus preached repentance as did John the Baptist, but soon he turned to preaching about the kingdom and the new order of morality that it would require, as seen in the sermon on the mount. He used many parables to indicate the nature of the kingdom; in what it was to consist and what it would require of those who would choose to enter into that kingdom. He performed many miracles and signs to prove that his mission was from God so as to move his hearers to put their faith and hope in him as the bearer of God's love and salvation to them. Near the end of his public ministry Jesus turned his attention towards training his apostles for their future work of spreading the good news and of establishing his Church, whereby his work of salvation would extend throughout the world.

As opposition to him increased, especially among the rulers of his people, Jesus began to warn his apostles about the final outcome of his life, that he was to suffer at the hands of the priests and scribes, be put to death and that he would rise again. This outcome for the Messiah was so contrary to what even the apostles expected that they did not know what to make of it. They did not know how to take his words or what they really meant. That is why they were utterly unprepared when it all happened and why they were so slow to believe in his Resurrection.

Mary surely recognized the growing opposition to Jesus and even if she had not been told about Jesus' prediction of his passion and death, she must have had some foreboding of the outcome. She knew the prophecies of Isaiah about the suffering servant, and no doubt, realized that they applied to the Messiah and hence to her son, Jesus. Being perfectly submissive to God's will all through her life, her submission was soon to be put to the supreme test.

3. The final accomplishment of our salvation: Christ's supreme hour began with the last supper: his last Paschal meal on earth with his disciples. It was a very solemn moment, but marred by the knowledge that he would be betrayed by one of his intimate friends, a betrayal he knew would be repeated by many of his chosen friends down the ages. Here we see the contrast between God's total gift of himself in love and man's blind, ungrateful, even malicious rejection of that love. The immensity of God's merciful love and goodness is never more revealed than when poured out upon those who are most undeserving and rebellious. That is the amazing contrast that runs through the whole drama of Christ's saving death: the immensity of God's limitless love for us and the enormity of man's blind ingratitude. The cruel death mankind inflicted on him, is used by Jesus as the means whereby he saves us from eternal death. We cannot fathom the depth of such love.

When Jesus was arrested the news must have been brought to Mary by the confused and fleeing apostles. From that moment Mary was intimately united with Jesus in spirit in a way we will never know in this life. As each detail of news about Jesus was brought to her the intensity of her love and compassion grew until she stood beneath the cross on Calvary.

Nature of sacrifice: Let us pause here and consider the nature of the act by which Jesus was to save mankind: the act of sacrifice. Sacrifice is regarded as the most perfect act of worship that can be given to God by a creature. That is why it is found in practically all primitive religions.

When man sees the greatness of God and his own utter dependence on God, man wants to give some concrete expression to the sentiments that vision of God arouses in his heart. Since words are inadequate, he wants to act out those sentiments in some concrete, sensible way. The most perfect way would be for him to immolate his own human life in witness to God's absolute rights over him. But seeing that God has given him his life for a reason and therefore does not desire this of him, man does what is next best. He takes things upon which his life depends and offers them as symbols of himself. That is why animals were immolated and burned, wine and milk poured. out and the burning of incense became so expressive. When sin entered into the world with the fall, reparation also became an important aspect of sacrifice.

Christ our sacrifice: Although God does not approve of human sacrifice, he made an exception in the case of his own divine Son. Jesus, now a member of our human race, was to be the sacrificial victim by which mankind would be freed from its debt of sin and restored to friendship with God. He was to be the one supreme sacrifice, symbolized by all the different kinds of sacrifice in the Old Testament, but especially by the Paschal Lamb. As the blood of the Paschal Lamb freed the Israelites from their bondage in Egypt, so the blood of Jesus was to free all mankind from the bondage of sin and Satan and open to us a passage into the promised inheritance of eternal life with God in heaven.

That supreme act of sacrifice took place on Calvary and we ourselves were there united with Jesus as his other self and bride in Mary. There we offered ourselves with him by giving our consent and acceptance through Mary. On Calvary Mary was no mere spectator; she was deeply involved in that supreme act of Jesus. She alone saw Calvary as a sacrifice; others saw it only as the cruel and unjust execution of an innocent man. Jesus alone is our Savior, for he alone was the priest and victim of sacrifice, offering himself as the head of all mankind to remove our debt of sin and reinstate us into friendship with his Father. But to do that he needed our consent and acceptance, and that is what Mary gave in the name of all mankind. Christ, by his saving death, could not have saved us if mankind were still in a state of refusing God's offer of friendship. Hence, just as Eve was united with Adam, as his bride, in refusing God's friendship, so Mary was united with Jesus, as his bride, in accepting God's new offer of his divine friendship. Mary is truly our co-redemptrix, united with Jesus in our restoration to new life even as Eve was united with Adam in bringing death upon mankind. As Mary's consent was necessary that Christ should become man at the Incarnation, so here also her consent, given in the name of all mankind, was necessary for mankind to receive the fruits of Christ's redemption.

In Adam mankind sinned by an act of disobedience inspired by pride; he sought his own life and well-being in himself, independent of God. To make reparation for that sin, Jesus, in contrast, acknowledged his total dependence on God in such a way as to sacrifice his human life in total submission to his Father's will, thus loving his Father more than himself. Being God, as well and man, this act of sacrifice of Jesus was of infinite value and so was more than adequate to make reparation for all the sins of mankind to the end of time. What is more, in that supreme act of sacrifice, Jesus united his humanity, and hence all of us his members, in that eternal act of love whereby in the Trinity he gives himself wholly to the Father in the Holy Spirit. In Jesus, in his humanity, we are made partakers of God's own divine life and nature. We are taken up with Jesus into the divine family of God as a girl wedded to the son of a king.

In this supreme sacrifice Jesus was acting as the head and leader of a new humanity, and therefore, as a social being united with his other self and bride in Mary. Jesus is the new Adam and Mary is the new Eve of a new race of mankind, a mankind now living by the very life of God himself. As Eve is the mother of the fallen human race Mary is the mother of a new redeemed human race. Through the divine life of grace, which we now have in Jesus, mankind has become a new creature, a new creation, a mankind living by the very life of God.

Every human being united with Jesus through sanctifying grace is living God's life; he is united with God who is all truth and goodness. He shares in God's own mutual knowledge and love which is the very life of the Trinity. That is the goal to which our whole being aspires, the peak of our existence: eternal life.

The marvel of the Mass: On Calvary Jesus ended his mortal life in the most supreme act of perfect love for his Father and, in that act of dying his humanity is fixed for all eternity. When Jesus, therefore, is made present on our altars by the words of consecration in the Mass, he is there present in that final and eternal act of love. He is present as our eternal sacrifice before the Father. In the Mass we have Calvary made present here and now so that we can unite ourselves with Jesus even as Mary did on Calvary in giving our consent and acceptance. The Mass is the greatest act on earth; therein all mankind is taken up into the very life of God in Jesus. In the Mass we are all united with Jesus in the very life of the Trinity, in his total gift of himself to his Father in the Holy Spirit.

St. Thomas Aquinas says that the "res" the "reality" present in the Eucharist is not just Jesus, but Jesus in his Mystical Body, his Church. Therefore, in the Mass all the members of Christ, the saints in heaven, the souls in purgatory and all the faithful on earth and even the angels, as creatures, are united with Jesus in his supreme gift of himself to the Father in the life of the Trinity. In the Mass we have heaven itself: the Trinity, all the angels and saints, and all the faithful on earth united with Jesus in giving ourselves eternally to the Father.

What Mary did in our place on Calvary we must now do by our own personal choice, for God will not save us without us. Hence, we must repent of our sins and accept Christ's salvation by being baptized into him, and then, strive to live with Jesus his life of friendship with his Father even as Mary did. The more perfectly we so unite ourselves with Jesus in living his life of love for the Father, the more fully will we share in the fruits of his redemption.

Salvation, man's call to friendship with God in the divine life, is now secure for mankind as a whole, but each individual man and woman must make it their own by a personal free choice. If Adam had not sinned, God's offer of friendship would have been secure for mankind as a whole, but each individual would still have been free to accept or reject it personally. It is much the same now with the redemption of Christ. The offer is secure for mankind, and cannot be lost, but each individual is free to accept or reject it.

D) THE FRUIT OF REDEMPTION: RESURRECTION AND ASCENSION

Our salvation was not complete without Christ's resurrection. On Calvary Jesus paid the debt of our sins, but was that payment accepted by God? That it was accepted became evident only with Christ's resurrection. That is why St. Paul could write, "If Christ is not risen, you are still in your sins." (1. Cor. 15:17) By raising Christ from the dead in his humanity to share his glory, God raised all mankind, in him, to friendship with himself. In Christ's resurrection God proclaims that all mankind is now in God's favor. Jesus himself bears witness to this when he said to Mary Magdalen, "Go tells my disciples that I ascend to My Father and to your Father, to My God and to your God." (Jn. 20: 17) God is now our Father even as he is Jesus' Father: he is now our God, even as he is Jesus' God. In Jesus we have been taken up into the divine family of God. In and with Jesus we now share in the eternal life of God himself.

After the death and burial of Jesus who can know the anguish of Mary's heart. And yet, great as her sorrow must have been, Mary was not without hope. The apostles saw Christ's death as the end of their dreams. To them everything had collapsed and was finished. But Mary, knowing that Jesus was the Messiah and what Scripture said of the suffering servant, knew that he would triumph in the end. She may not have known that his triumph would be through his resurrection, unless the apostles had told her about Christ's prediction of his death and resurrection.

When the disciple, John, took Mary into his home, right after the burial of Jesus, they must have talked about the pain and bewilderment of all that had taken place so suddenly. And surely Mary must have passed on to John something of her hope in Jesus' eventual triumph. I like to think: that is why John was the first of the apostles to believe in the resurrection when he entered the empty tomb after Peter. He had been prepared for it by Mary.

Did Jesus appear to Mary: Did Jesus appear first to Mary on the morning of his resurrection? Many of the Fathers of the Church believe that he did. I find it impossible to think otherwise, and even that he appeared to her before all others. If it is not mentioned in the Gospel, that is because Mary was not to be a public witness before the world as were the apostles. However, knowing that Jesus was the most loving of all sons, he could not have done otherwise than share his triumph with his mother who had shared so deeply in his sufferings. If the night of suffering comes before the dawn, then Mary who suffered most with Jesus in his passion and death, deserved to rejoice before all others on that victorious dawn of Easter day.

The empty tomb: If Mary retained hope in Christ's final victory that certainly was not true of the apostles. All the Gospel accounts show them as utterly unprepared for Christ's resurrection.

They met every report with disbelief. Christ's passion and death shattered their idea that the Messiah would found an earthly kingdom. Indeed that idea was still with them up to the moment of Christ's Ascension when they asked him, "Lord, has the time come? Are you going to restore the kingdom of Israel?" (Acts 1:6) Only when the apostles had direct personal contact with Jesus did they believe, and even then doubts arose in their minds. They had to touch him and even see him eat before they were convinced. Thomas, who refused to accept the word of the other apostles until he had direct contact with Jesus himself, is a perfect picture of their slowness to expect the Resurrection.

In the light of the Gospel accounts, it is difficult to see how some Catholic scholars can question the bodily resurrection of Jesus, claiming that it was some kind of spiritual experience of the apostles who were convinced that Jesus would somehow come back. The Gospels show them as being convinced of the very opposite. Apparently, such scholars do not want to accept the possibility of miracles. If they do not believe in Christ's bodily resurrection, how can they believe in the creed which states, "I believe in the resurrection of the body?" If all mankind is to rise from the dead on the last day, why should not Jesus have been the first of all the dead to rise, as St. Paul says of him.

The Ascension: Forty days after his resurrection Jesus ascended into heaven. Was Mary present on this occasion? She is not mentioned as being present, but it is difficult to think that she was not, especially as we find her right afterwards with the apostles and others in the upper room awaiting the coming of the Holy Spirit. Jesus could not have left her out of such an important event: his final leave-taking that would entail his visible separation from her for many years to come. It is very likely that Jesus told Mary beforehand that he would leave her on earth for many years, as being needed by her new children, even preparing her for their separation.

Mary must have rejoiced to know that Jesus was going to the Father to receive his rightful glory, but the separation was still very painful. But, as always, Mary was perfectly docile to the divine will. Jesus left Mary on earth to mother the infant Church. However, she was not to have any office or public role in the Church itself or in the ministry of the apostles. Mary was to be in the heart of the Church: a source of strength, encouragement and inspiration to the apostles and early Christians. She was to be the contemplative, ever united with her Son in spirit, winning all those graces for the early Church which contributed to its rapid growth throughout the world.

CHAPTER III

MARY IN THE CHURCH: THE MYSTICAL BODY OF CHRIST

With his Ascension Jesus departed from our world in his visible bodily presence. As he said, "It is expedient for you that I go because, unless I go, the advocate will not come." (Jn. 16:7) However, Jesus had promised to remain with them to the end of time: "I will not leave you orphans: I will come back to you." (Jn. 14:18) And, "Know that I am with you always, yes to the end of time." (Mt. 28:20) Jesus departs in his physical presence, but he is to remain with us by a spiritual presence through the Holy Spirit. As he said, "The kingdom of God is within you." (Lk. 17:21) Indeed, since spiritual realities are higher than those that are physical, Jesus is now present to us in a higher and more perfect way than when he walked on earth.

But still, Christ's spiritual presence in our midst is to have its physical embodiment, in the institutional Church. In the Incarnation Jesus took to himself a physical human body; now he takes to himself a social body, the Church. And in that Church he is still with us; teaching, guiding, and sanctifying us even more perfectly than during his physical presence on earth. Mary had an essential role in Christ's physical coming into the world at the Incarnation and in his saving work of redemption. Now she is to have an essential role in Christ's spiritual presence in the Church, and in the application of the fruits of Christ's redemption down the ages.

In this Chapter I will first consider the founding of the Church at Pentecost and then the nature of the Church as Christ himself, still present in our midst in his Mystical Body. I will then consider Mary's place in the Church, which is something real and profound, but also something full of mystery.

A) PENTECOST AND THE FOUNDING OF THE CHURCH

Pentecost: the coming of the Holy Spirit upon the apostles, is generally considered to be the moment when the Church was founded as a visible social reality. But its invisible inner spiritual reality, the life of grace, giving man access to God's divine life of friendship, actually came into being with Jesus' passion, death and Resurrection.

After the Ascension, the apostles assembled in the upper room to await the coming of the Holy Spirit, as Jesus had told them to do. With them were Mary and other men and women to the number of about 120. (cf. Acts 1:15) They were all united in prayer awaiting the coming of the Holy Spirit promised by Jesus. As Mary had an essential role in the work of our salvation so here too in the coming of the Holy Spirit

The Holy Spirit comes on the apostles through Mary: From the way St. Luke describes the event, some of the Fathers of the Church have held that the Holy Spirit descended, first upon Mary, and then spread out on the disciples so that they received the Holy Spirit as coming upon them through Mary. Their reasoning is based on the text, "Something appeared to them that seemed like tongues of fire; these separated and came to rest on the heads of each one." (Acts 2:3) These tongues of fire were first united, presumably over Mary, and only then did they separate and go and rest on the heads of each person who was present. This was very symbolic of the new role of Mary's Motherhood. She is to be the mother of Jesus in his social nature: his Mystical Body, the Church. The words of Jesus on the cross, "Woman this is your son," are here given their concrete fulfillment.

The Church received its visible inauguration at Pentecost and it is only then that we hear of baptism being given to those who believed in the words of Peter. From then on all those who accepted the Good News were always baptized and received the Holy Spirit. We do not hear of Mary or the apostles being baptized or even those who were in the upper room when the Holy Spirit came upon them. No doubt they were baptized by the Holy Spirit in an immediate way without the formal sacrament itself, which, of course, God is always free to do.

Mary after Pentecost: After Pentecost we have no longer any official record of Mary's life. It is believed that she lived for some twenty years afterwards. Mary's place will now be in the heart of the Church: a place far more important and all-embracing. She will also be the mother of the Church and hence, a source of great encouragement to the apostles and a beautiful example in living the new Christian life. It must have been through her prayerful union with Jesus that obtain much of the great successes and rapid growth witnessed in the early Church.

We have every reason also to believe that Matthew and Luke received their information for the infancy narratives in their Gospels from Mary as their source, whether direct or indirect. Since Mary was living with John, the apostles and early Christians surely turned to Mary in their desire to know more about Jesus, especially about the years that preceded his public ministry.

B) THE NATURE OF THE CHURCH

What is the Church? The Church is Jesus Christ, his Mystical Body. It is Christ in his social nature. Just as Jesus took to himself an individual human nature in the Incarnation, so now he has taken to himself a social nature, all regenerated mankind, into a living unity with himself, like branches in a vine. The Church, then, is an extension of the Incarnation. It is Christ united with all his members in one social and living reality. That is why we can say, "Christ is the Church," "Mary is the Church," "The Faithful are the Church." We all form one and the same living and organic reality that is Christ. That too is why whatever we do to one of the members of Jesus we do to Jesus and also to ourselves.

The test of faith asked of those, living at the time of Christ, was that they believe in him as the Messiah sent by God. Christ was always asking for that faith in the Gospels. But the test of faith for those who are living today is that we believe in Christ as present and living in his Church. We must believe that the Church is *Christ himself* still teaching us the truth, guiding us in how to live our lives and sanctifying us through his grace contained in the sacraments of the Church. The Church is Christ himself still present with us through his Spirit. That is why the Church, in its mission as teacher, is as infallible as Christ himself. Without that faith in Jesus present in his Church, one is not a believing Christian, much less a believing Catholic. Those who reject that faith are no different from those who, in the time of Christ, denied that he was the Messiah.

Christ in his human nature was a composite of a visible material body and an invisible spiritual soul. Now in his social nature, his Mystical Body, the Church, he also has a visible body: the institutional Church, and an invisible soul: the divine life of sanctifying grace. It is by this life of sanctifying grace that the Holy Spirit lives in all the members of Christ, even as he lived in Christ as man when on earth.

Every social institution is made up of a visible element: the members united under some form of leadership, and an invisible element: some intentional goal, such as brotherhood, mountain-climbing, bird-watching, whatever. Hence, the Church, as a social institution, also has its visible element and its invisible element. I would now like to consider these more in detail.

The visible element of the Church: The visible element of the Church is its visible institution. It consists in the social unity of all the baptized faithful under the leadership of one appointed by Christ himself to be its visible head, Peter, the Pope. It is a human institution made up of men and women who are united in faith and love with Christ under his visible Vicar, the Pope. The subordinate leaders and ministers in this institution are bishops and priests who today promote its visible goal, by teaching the truth, administering the sacraments and guiding the faithful infallibly under the leadership of Christ in his Vicar. This visible social institution was inaugurated at Pentecost for it was then that the apostles began to preach the Good News, baptize the believers and guide them according to the will of Christ.

Down the ages this visible institute has developed under the guidance of the Holy Spirit, like every other social institution, according as needs arose, until it is what it is seen to be today. It is Christ himself, but it is not without its human limitations. However, because Christ is guiding and protecting his Church, none of these limitations can hinder its essential mission of guiding mankind infallibly, in the areas of faith and morals, so as to obtain salvation.

The invisible element of the Church: The invisible element of the Church is its inner life: the unity of all the faithful forming one living organism with Christ. We are like branches all sharing in the life of the vine or like living cells sharing in the life of the body. Each cell in our body has its own individual life yet all are united in the one life of the body. In the same way all the faithful live by the one divine life that is in Christ.

Sanctifying grace: The inner life we have in Christ is sanctifying grace. While sanctifying grace is a mystery above our full comprehension, let us see what we can know about it. In sanctifying grace there is something created and something uncreated. It is a kind of union between God and the creature somewhat as man himself is a union between matter and spirit. Sanctifying grace is something created in that it effects a certain adaptation in the soul of man. If an animal were given to possess rational life, its body would have to be adapted with a tongue, and hands and the like to met the requirements proper to that new life. However, the gift of rational life itself would be something very substantial and supernatural, something far superior to its animal life.

In much the same way, for us to possess the divine life of God, our soul or life principle, needs to be adapted by certain qualities in order to live the higher life of God. These added qualities are the theological virtues of Faith, Hope and Charity, the infused moral virtues and the gifts of the Holy Spirit. By these adaptations in our intellectual powers we are capable of being united with God and participate in God's own divine life. But the uncreated reality in sanctifying grace is the Holy Spirit, God himself. As St. Paul says, "The charity of Christ is poured into our hearts by the Holy Spirit who is given to us." (Rom. 5:5)

In sanctifying grace God himself, the Holy Spirit, becomes the source and principle of the life in Christ's Mystical Body. That is why Pope Pius XII, in his encyclical on the Mystical Body, says that the Holy Spirit is the soul of the Mystical Body. Just as in the Incarnation the divine nature is united with human nature in the person of Christ, so here the divine life, God's mutual love, the Holy Spirit, is united with our human life in a mysterious way in the person of Christ. Christ's human life and hence, the human life of all his members, is given a participation in the divine life of God, much as Christ's humanity participated in the works of Christ's divinity.

What that participation is like is often compared to iron plunged into fire. The iron glows with the beauty of the fire itself and shares in all the energy and warmth of fire, but it never becomes fire. Thus it is that through sanctifying grace we share in the very beauty and power of God as though we were God himself, wholly immersed in God, yet we always remain a mere creature in our nature.

Difference between the Church and other social groups: Externally the Church is much like any other human social institution. However, the Church differs from these other social groups in that its inner unifying principle is not something merely intentional, as in other human societies, but a unified life that is a real participation in the very life of God himself. As our body participates in the intellectual life of our soul through seeing, hearing, speaking and making things, so we, through sanctifying grace, participate in the divine life of God. Our body could not participate more in our intellectual life without itself becoming intellectual nor can we participate more in the divine life of God, through sanctifying grace, without ourselves becoming divine.

There is, then, only one life flowing through all the members of Christ's Mystical Body, the Church, whereby we form one living organic reality: the very life of God. Through sanctifying grace we are united with Jesus as though forming one living person. All that we do according to the guidance of Christ's Spirit within us is really done by Jesus and is of infinite value. That is why, through grace, we can merit an eternal and infinite reward in strict justice before God. When we act contrary to the will of God, we are like sick or paralyzed members who do not respond to the will of their living agent. Hence, such actions cannot be attributed to Christ, but only to ourselves. Also, since we are one living reality in Christ, whatever we do to one another we do to Christ himself, and so we will be judged on the last day. (Mt. 25)

No salvation outside the Church: Since we are one with Christ only as members in his Mystical Body, the Church, there is no salvation outside the Church. Christ alone is our mediator who, in the Church, unites us with God. Of course this unity with Christ refers essentially to the inner life of the Church and not necessarily to the external institutional Church. One can be united with Jesus through sanctifying grace while not a member of his visible Church should he be unaware of the necessity of Church membership for salvation. However, should such a one come to recognize his obligation to be a member of the visible Church, and refused, he would no longer be obedient to God's will and would then be without sanctifying grace.

C) MARY'S PLACE IN THE CHURCH

As Mary was closely united with Jesus in his personal human life, so she is closely united with Jesus in his social life within his Church. St. Paul sees the Church as the bride of Christ (cf. Eph. 5:25), but Mary too is the bride of Christ. She is the new Eve united with Jesus as his other self, in the work of our salvation. Throughout her life Mary experienced in herself what the Church was to experience later. Before the Church existed Mary was holy and immaculate and united with Jesus in mutual knowledge and love. Before the Church reaches its goal of unity with Christ, Mary will already be raised up to heaven in both body and soul. All that Mary was before the Church existed the Church itself must gradually come to experience in herself. Like Mary the Church seeks to become holy and immaculate; she seeks to share in the mysteries of Christ and to be raised up in him to glory. Mary is thus the first member of the Church in whom, by anticipation, the Church realizes in all its absolute perfection its true goal of becoming one with Jesus as his spouse.

Thus we see that there exists a real likeness between Mary and the Church which implies a certain unity between them that is, however, shrouded in mystery. We can actually say, "Mary is the Church," and "The Church is Mary," but we cannot explain all that is implied in those two statements. Let us see what we can know of this mystery.

Mary and the Church are one: Scheeben in his book, *The Virgin Mother of the Savior,* likens the unity between Mary and the Church to what theologians call "Circumincession:" that unity within the Trinity whereby the three divine persons exist in one another. We find that unity expressed in those words of Jesus, "He who sees me sees the Father," and in his answer to Philip, "Do you not believe that I am in the Father and the Father is in me." (Jn. 14:10) Therefore, just as we cannot entirely understand how the three divine persons exist in one another, so neither can we understand how Mary and the Church are one. However, by using some comparisons we can see something of its reality.

The unity of Mary with the Church is much like the unity that exists between our body and soul: while our body is something visible and our soul invisible they both make up one united being. The Church is the kingdom of God which Jesus came to establish on earth. The visible reality of that kingdom is the institutional Church while its inner invisible reality: its inner life, Christ's life of grace, is fully found in Mary. All that the Church is in an external way Mary is in its inner life. The grace which the Church possesses and dispenses to the faithful in an external way through the sacraments, Mary possesses and dispenses interiorly as a loving mother and as the Mediatrix of all graces.

The Church, being a living spiritual reality, must exist in a person. Jesus is the person of the Church as its head and bridegroom, but Mary is the person of the Church as its bride. Both are united in a perfect spiritual union of love as bridegroom and bride, and all the faithful are called to be united with Jesus their bridegroom in and through Mary, his perfect bride.

This mutual relationship between Jesus, Mary and the faithful is best conveyed by the comparison used by St. Paul, who likens the Church, Christ's Mystical Body, to a human being. Therein Jesus is the head, the Church, and therefore Mary, are his body, and the faithful are its members united with Jesus through and in his body. Here again, we see how Mary and the Church are regarded as one. Whatever the members receive from the head comes to them through the body which possesses in itself everything that eventually is found in the different individual members. Mary and the Church possess the fullness of all the gifts of grace and glory Christ has won for mankind, and every individual Christian receives and shares in those riches externally through the institutional Church and internally through Mary's mediation.

Scripture itself, in several texts also implies that Mary and the Church are one. St. Paul tells us that the Church is the bride of Christ which he "Made clean by washing her in water and a form of words, so that when he takes her to himself, she would be glorious without spot or wrinkle or anything like that, but wholly spotless." (Eph. 5:27) These words, as applied to a person, can only be true of Mary. Therefore, when they are applied to the Church it is as being one with Mary in some way.

In the book of Revelation, the "Woman adorned with the sun and standing on the moon with twelve stars on her head for a crown in the pangs of giving birth," (Rev. 12:1-2) is seen as an image of both Mary and the Church. Mary gives birth to the faithful in a spiritual way by mediating divine grace, and the Church gives birth to the faithful in an external way through baptism. Since Satan cannot harm Mary or the Church in themselves, he therefore goes in pursuit of their children, the faithful. It is just this hidden unity that exists between Mary and the Church that moved the Fathers of Vatican II to treat Mary within the document on the Church and not in a separate document as some had desired.

The fact that we say, "Mary is the Church" and "Mary is the mother of the Church" does not imply any conflict but only points to a mystery. It is much the same when we say "Jesus is God" and "Jesus is the Son of God." The fact that Mary and the Church are one does not prevent them from differing even as our body and soul differ while remaining one in being.

Now Mary and the Church are alike: Mary and the Church are alike in that both are mothers: the Church is a mother by giving birth to the faithful through baptism and by nourishing, guiding and healing them through her magisterium and the administration of the sacraments. Mary is a mother by the fact of giving birth to Jesus and hence to his members, the faithful. She is also a mother in that she cooperated with Jesus in giving us birth into God's divine life on Calvary. Indeed it was on Calvary that Jesus confirmed her title as our mother when he said to his apostle John, "This is your mother." (Jn. 19:27)

Mary and the Church are both the bride and spouse of Jesus. St. Paul implies that the Church is the bride of Christ, when in his epistle to the Ephesians he sees the Church as the spotless bride that Jesus has taken to himself. Mary is the bride of Jesus as being intimately united with Jesus as his other self, in the work of our redemption.

Mary and the Church are alike in other respects. As the Church is always docile to the Holy Spirit in its essential mission of teaching and sanctifying, so Mary was always docile to the Holy Spirit in her personal life. As the Church is holy and spotless in her faith and love, so Mary is holy and spotless in her personal life of faith and love. As Eve was taken from the side of Adam, so Mary and the Church were taken from the side of Christ: an observation made by some Fathers of the Church.

How Mary and the Church differ: Mary and the Church differ especially in that the Church is found in the external structure of Christ's Mystical Body, whereas Mary is found in its invisible life. The Church and Mary also differ in the way they participate in the life of Jesus. The Church participates in his life by acting in his name through the external works of teaching, guiding and sanctifying. Mary participates in the life of Jesus by living his inner life of mutual knowledge and love for his Father and by promoting that same life in the faithful as the Mediatrix of all grace.

Wherein Mary and the Church differ they really complement one another, much as our body and soul complement each other. While Mary and the Church differ in their particular functions in the body of Christ, they are united in striving for the same goal. Both seek to unite all mankind with God in the divine life as present in Jesus, our one and only mediator with God. A final point of difference between Mary and the Church is that the institutional Church will cease to exist at the end of time, but its inner life, in Mary, will remain for all eternity.

Because of the hidden unity between Mary and the Church we can say that, before Pentecost, the Church was hidden in Mary and now, since Pentecost, Mary is hidden in the Church. While the Church is perfect in its mission of acting in the name of Jesus, Mary is perfect in living the inner life of Jesus with his Father and in promoting that life in all the faithful. As the Church comes to know itself more perfectly, at the same time, it comes to know Mary more perfectly. In Mary it finds its initial golden age, in her Immaculate Conception, and it foresees its final golden age, in her bodily Assumption into heaven. The more the Church recognizes her own limitations and imperfections, the more she recognizes in Mary her perfect ideal and model. The more the Church honors Mary as the perfect image and model of what she herself should become, the more the Church discovers the value of Mary's mediation. This surely explains why there has been such a notable development of Marian dogmas in recent centuries.

CHAPTER IV

MARY IN HEAVEN AND AS MEDIATRIX OF ALL GRACES

After Pentecost we have no official record of Mary's life, but we do have some apocryphal writings which may or may not contain some authentic traditional beliefs. We cannot be sure of what Mary's life was like after Pentecost, but we do know that she lived under the care of the apostle John. We can also be sure they shared with each other their knowledge and experience of Jesus. Mary must have been a wonderful inspiration to the apostles and to the early Christian believers and also a great source of counsel and encouragement. Since she was given no place in the apostolic ministry, her main occupation was that of living a contemplative life of union with Jesus. By that prayerful union with Jesus she won for the early Church its outstanding growth and successes. When the time came for her to leave this world for heaven, her prayer and work, in the Mystical Body of Christ, took on a new phase. She then became the Queen of Heaven and the Mediatrix of all graces.

In this chapter I will consider the question of Mary's death and Assumption, her role as Queen of Heaven and her mission as Mediatrix of all graces.

A) MARY'S DEATH AND ASSUMPTION

That Mary has been taken up body and soul into heaven is now a dogma of faith. However, Pius XII, in defining the dogma of Mary's Assumption, deliberately left open the question as to whether Mary actually died or whether she was taken bodily into heaven without experiencing the separation of body and soul in death. There are arguments for both sides of this question.

l. Did Mary die or not? In Scripture it is quite evident that God willed the death of his Son as the means for our salvation. However, any human act of Christ was of infinite value and could have merited our salvation. If God willed that our salvation should depend on the death of his Divine Son, this was no capricious choice on God's part. Mersch in his book, *The Theology of the Mystical Body,* says that it was because death is man's final and perfect act and that, therefore, Christ had to be perfect man, above all in that final and supreme act of man's life: death. If that was true of Christ, then it would appear that it should also be true of Mary and every other human being. This is one of the strongest arguments favoring the opinion that Mary passed through the portals of death like the rest of mankind.

However, we find that there are good reasons why Mary should have been an exception to this rule. Mankind became subject to death only after the sin of our first parents. If they had not sinned each individual man would have terminated his life in this world by some kind of final act that would not have involved death. We can only guess at what that act might have been: perhaps some kind of trance or ecstasy. However, since Mary was redeemed by prevention, it would appear only fitting that she should be exempted from this penalty of original sin. If she was preserved from the far greater penalty, as the loss of grace, why not also from its lesser penalties, including death. Christ had to pass through death because, having taken upon himself the burden of our sins, he had to suffer the full consequence of those sins. But this was not the case with Mary. Mary's death was not necessary for her to be our co-redeemer nor was it even desirable, since it would appear to detract from Christ's work as our sole redeemer. Mary was united with Jesus in his saving death as a consenting and willing recipient and not as one meriting her own salvation in any strict sense.

That Mary should have been given the privilege of not dying appears all the more likely since as St. Paul tells us, those who are still alive at Christ's final coming will not experience death. He writes, "Those who have died in Christ will be the first to rise and then those of us who are still alive will be taken up into the clouds together with them to meet the Lord in the air. (1 Thes. 4:17)

Christ, by his death has freed us from all the consequences of original sin, but we do not receive all these fruits at the same moment in time. Some, its spiritual effects, we receive at baptism, others, like freedom from concupiscence, suffering and death, we will receive only on the last day. That is why those living at the time of general resurrection will be free from death without having to experience it. There is no reason then, why Mary who was free from all the other consequences of original sin, by way of prevention, should not also have been freed from that of dying. The only consequence of original sin that Mary and Jesus experienced is that of suffering. But suffering in itself does not imply any blemish, but is rather a most powerful means of expressing love. If Jesus took upon himself the supreme suffering of death, it was that he might be the savior of mankind.

2. Mary's Assumption: That Mary was free from the penalty of death is a privilege we would be happy to know was granted to her, although it may never become a dogma of faith. But Mary's bodily Assumption is now a dogma of faith and has great importance for us. Like Christ's own Resurrection and Ascension it proves that we too will one day reign in glory united with Jesus in our own glorified bodies. It is only fitting that Christ, now reigning in heaven, should be there in the fullness, not only of his individual humanity, but also in the fullness of his social humanity with his other self in Mary. In heaven, Christ should be complete in his glorified humanity, both as individual and as social, and only awaiting that final fullness when all his members will be united with him in likeness to, and in union with Mary.

Since Mary's bodily Assumption is now a dogma of faith we must believe that after some final event in her life, she was taken up into heaven, body and soul. We have no reliable historical account of that event although the term used in the early Church to express Mary's departure, "Dormitio" (sleep), gives us some grounds for accepting, as a traditional belief, that Mary did not pass through death. Also, we have no precise Scriptural text we can use to prove Mary's Assumption. The belief in her Assumption, like that of her Immaculate Conception, rests more on tradition, and on the Church's reflection on Mary's place in the work of redemption as revealed in Scripture as a whole, than on any precise text. As the Holy Spirit inspired the faithful to believe in Mary's Assumption from the dawn of devotion to Mary in the early Church, so he has now inspired the Magisterium to declare it a dogma of faith. Here we find the Holy Spirit guiding the Church, not so much in the interpretation of any precise text, but rather in her understanding of the overall message contained in Scripture.

B) MARY AS QUEEN OF HEAVEN

Mary is given the title of Queen of Heaven and indeed Queen of both men and angels. But Mary is not the Queen of angels in the same sense that she is Queen of men. An earthly queen is queen of the subjects of the kingdom because she enjoys sovereign authority with the king. But she is queen, in the fullest sense, only over her own children whom She has begotten for the king. Hence Mary is Queen of the angels in the first sense but of men in the second sense, as being their mother in giving them the divine life of sanctifying grace.

1. Mary as Queen of Angels: How Mary exercises her Queenly authority over the angels is not too clear, for our knowledge of the angelic world is very limited. Certainly they act as ministering angels for Mary even as they do for God in serving the needs of mankind. As Queen of Heaven Mary is more closely united with God, and hence, she has a deeper insight into the mysteries of God than the angels. Because of this, Mary can pass on her higher knowledge to the angels even as the higher angels pass on their knowledge to the lower ones, as St. Thomas Aquinas teaches. Hence, the angels love Mary as a Queen who gives them to know the secrets of the King ever more fully and as ever increasing their own beatitude in God.

2. Mary as Queen of men: Mary is the Queen of men in the fullest sense by having cooperated with Jesus in giving us birth into the divine life on Calvary. However, she exercises her Queenship over those who are on earth differently from those who are in heaven. For those on earth she is the Mediatrix of all graces, seeking to bring all her children into the most perfect possible union of friendship with Jesus, who is her own most beloved spouse.

For those who have passed into the next life, the exercise of her Queenship must differ somewhat for those who have just left this world and those who are in the fullness of heavenly glory. For those who have just departed from this life, it is said that Mary presents each one of them to Jesus and pleads their cause, as we would expect of any loving mother. She is also said to be very solicitous for her children in Purgatory, praying for them, encouraging them, soothing their pain, and joyfully bringing them into heaven when their period of purgation is complete.

Mary's joy in doing all this is certainly greater than the individual's own joy. Mary has the happiness of rejoicing with both Jesus and the blessed person in that happy and eternal encounter.

In what Mary's Queenship consists for those now reigning with her in heaven and for all the saints after the general resurrection it is more difficult to know. For one thing it will certainly consist in sharing with the saints her higher knowledge of the mysteries of God as she does with the angels. Then there will be the mutual joy Mary will have in being the mother of so many beautiful children and the joy each soul will experience in having such a wonderful Mother and Queen. We may even wonder who will be the happier: Mary in being our mother or we in having such a loving mother. Like the Little Flower, St Therese of Lisieux, we will feel ourselves to be the more fortunate since we will have a blessed Mother but Mary will not.

In heaven Mary will mediate all God's gifts to us in some way. As parents share everything with their children so Jesus and Mary will share their eternal joy and happiness with us, their children. Jesus will share with us all his merits and glory and even his divine Sonship with his Father. Mary will share with us her virginal purity, her great love for Jesus and even her Immaculate Conception. St. Paul says that when Jesus takes his Church to himself "She will be glorious and without spot or wrinkle but holy and faultless." If this applies to the Church then it applies to all of us its members. We will share in Mary's own purity and Immaculate Conception. In Mary we will love Jesus and be loved by Jesus and in Jesus we will love the Father and be loved by the Father in their mutual bond of love, the Holy Spirit. Then that twofold friendship to which we are called, with Jesus as man and with Jesus as God, will be perfectly attained.

C) MARY AS MEDIATRIX OF ALL GRACES

For those who are still on earth, Mary exercises her Queenship, as the Mediatrix of all graces. That Mary mediates some of God's graces to us we cannot doubt, for even we can mediate God's grace to others in various ways, for example, by preaching, praying, healing, teaching, to mention only a few. What makes Mary's mediation something special is that she has been given the privilege of mediating all God's graces. No grace comes to us from Jesus that does not pass through Mary's motherly hands.

Some persons do not want to grant this privilege to Mary because it seems to detract from Jesus' role as our sole mediator with God. But there is no conflict here. Jesus is our sole mediator with God, and Mary is our sole Mediatrix with Jesus. As Jesus alone can unite us perfectly with God in divine friendship, so Mary alone can unite us perfectly with Jesus in human friendship.

In this section, I would like to consider first the various reasons why Mary is rightly said to be the Mediatrix of all graces. Then I will consider how she exercises her role as Mediatrix in our regard. And, since Mary's life has had various stages, we will need to consider how she has or does exercise her mediation in those different stages of her life.

1. Reasons for Mary's title of Mediatrix of all graces: Mary mediates some grace, but that she actually mediates every grace that is given to every individual person is a privilege many would like to see become a defined dogma of faith. Let us see what grounds there are for that possibility.

Mary's first title to being the Mediatrix of all graces is her divine Motherhood. Having given us Jesus, fount of all grace, she is, indirectly, the Mediatrix of all the graces we receive from that fount. Not only did Mary give us Jesus, the fount of all grace, she also was perfectly united with Him in winning all the graces of which he is the fount. Therefore, all that Jesus has won for us in strict justice, Mary has won for us by a certain fitness. Without her consent and acceptance to Christ's saving death, as the new Eve, we could not have been saved or restored to God's life of friendship. It is only fitting then, that she who helped win the fullness of graces given to mankind, should also have a role in the application of these graces to all who receive them.

Then too, Mary is a kind of reservoir of all graces, for she alone has received in herself the total fullness of all the graces Jesus has won for mankind. Hence, whoever receives grace from Christ receives them from Mary's fullness. Did not the angel at the Annunciation hail her as "Full of grace?"

The above reasons show us how fitting it is that Mary should be the universal Mediatrix of all grace, but the final reason can only be: that God has willed it so. Although God has not expressed that will in so many words, yet it would appear that he has indicated his will by the role he has given Mary in all the crucial events in Christ's life. At the Annunciation her "Fiat" gave Christ to the world. At the Visitation it was Mary who brought Jesus to John the Baptist, that John might be sanctified in his mother's womb. At Cana it was through Mary that Jesus was moved to begin his public ministry. On Calvary she consented to and accepted Jesus' work of salvation in the name of all mankind. At Pentecost the Holy Spirit come upon the apostles and the church through Mary.

Because of these examples in the life of Jesus, and because of their own experience of Mary's place in their own spiritual lives, many saints have come to recognize this will of God. St. Bernard was so convinced of its reality that he stated emphatically, "It is the will of God that we should receive all things through Mary."

That God has willed to give Mary the privilege of dispensing all his graces to the children of men would seem to be necessary for the perfect fulfillment of God's goal in creating. God's reason for creating was to share his own happiness with others, in the highest possible way. But God's happiness consists in giving and sharing all he has. Hence, he must give someone the power of doing just that; of being able to take all the gifts God can possibly give a creature and to give them to others in their turn. This God has made possible to Mary and to the Church: to the Church in an external way and to Mary in an internal way. Mary and the Church alone have received the fullness of all God's spiritual gifts and that fullness they have the privilege of imparting to others, and through others back to God himself. Hence, in Mary and in the Church, we and all mankind have the blessing of giving to others and back to God himself all that God has given to mankind.

Here I should mention that although God can and does sometimes dispense his graces without the instrumentality of the institutional Church, he never does so without Mary's mediation, because he never has a reason for doing so, since she is perfectly united with him in heaven.

2. How Mary exercises her mediation: Once we are willing to accept that Mary is truly the Mediatrix of all graces, we will want to know how she fulfills her role as Mediatrix. Certainly it will be in the likeness of a mother caring for her most loved children. If human mothers can love their children with such tender and self-sacrificing love, Mary, who has been given the privilege of sharing and revealing God's own motherliness, will far excel the love of all other mothers. No one will be excluded from her maternal solicitude, especially the weak and the poor. That is why she is the refuge of sinners. No one can better reassure and smooth their way back to Jesus than Mary, the mother of God. Her love will embrace every detail in our lives; she will never let us out of her sight nor shall we ever be beyond the reach of her motherly solicitude. Since Jesus himself is her supreme love, her one desire and goal will be to present us to Jesus as perfect and beautiful as she can possibly help us to become.

Indeed, she will love and care for us as she did for Jesus himself; she will see us as her Jesus, as one of his members. All the riches and treasures of grace that Jesus has put into her hands she will use to nurture, train and educate us so that we may become a perfect likeness to Jesus himself. She will see us as a gift of Jesus' love to her: that she might care for us, and then, offer us back to Jesus as a gift of her love for him.

In giving us Mary as the Mediatrix of all his graces, Jesus has given us a mother in our spiritual lives so that we might be no less provided for than in our natural human life. We need the complementary help of father and mother in our human life: so too in our spiritual life. Christians who do not acknowledge Mary's place in their spiritual lives are like children of a single parent, they lack something necessary, for their full spiritual development.

3. The means by which Mary exercises her mediation: Let us now consider what means Mary has at her disposal for applying God's grace to us. One of these is certainly her power of intercession with Jesus. Jesus is the one and only source of every grace, but he has appointed Mary as his universal almoner so that she can obtain everything she asks from him for all her children. That is why Mary is said to be the "Omnipotent Supplex" (Omnipotent by supplication) because Jesus can refuse her nothing she asks of him.

Mary's power to help us, is not limited to her intercession. She herself actually applies to us in a very personal and motherly way all that she obtains from Jesus for us. And she does this, as the theologian would say "as a conjoined instrument:" as a tool in the hands of a craftsman. So Jesus used his humanity, as a conjoined instrument of his divinity, in the working of miracles and in uttering prophecies. But, Mary is a person who is united with Jesus as a conjoined instrument; hence, it is really Jesus himself who is caring for us through the motherliness of Mary. As Jesus could say, "It is the Father living in me who is doing this work," (Jn. 14:10) so Mary can say, "It is Jesus living in me who is loving and caring for you."

If some saints were given the power to work miracles according to their own judgment and choice, as is certainly said of St. Bernard, how much more should not Mary have been given the power to dispense God's gifts to us according to her own motherly love and solicitude. Does not the mother in the family use the income of her husband according to her own judgment and choice in caring for her household and her children? Surely Mary is not given less authority in caring for God's spiritual household: the Church and all the faithful.

However, since Mary is perfectly united with Jesus in love, all that she does in our regard is always in perfect conformity with God's will. Hence, she is guided, not only by her own love for us, but also by God's love for us so that she has the joy of ministering God's infinite love for us as well as her own personal love. Because Mary is always guided by the divine will in all she does, she can never make a mistake in her loving care for us. We are as secure in Mary's hands as we are in those of God himself.

A practical difficulty: There is a practical difficulty here with regard to Mary's mediation: "How can she personally dispense each and every grace given to every individual human being at every moment throughout the whole world?" How can a mere creature have the capacity to give her undivided attention to millions of people at one and the same time? All we can say is that God must be able to give such a capacity to Mary and hence, to any intellectual creature. In practice, the faithful certainly believe that Mary has such a capacity. When thousands take part in a pilgrimage to one of her shrines, each individual surely believes that when he prays to Mary, he or she, has Mary's full and undivided attention. If God can give man the power to use created elements in building a computer that can handle billions of bits of information in a few seconds, he can surely make a spiritual and intellectual being that can do that and even more. Spirits are not limited as are bodily and material beings. Hence, we need not fear that in heaven we will have any difficulty in communicating with the myriads of saints and angels that abide there.

4. Different periods of Mary's mediation: In God's eternal plan for creation, Mary has always had her role as our Mediatrix with Jesus, but in different ways, according to the different unfolding stages of that plan. Certainly before her birth Mary could not act as our Mediatrix in any real sense. However, since grace given in the Old Testament by reason of the foreseen merits of Jesus and since Mary had a passive yet essential role in obtaining those graces, she can, in this way, be said to be the Mediatrix of those graces given in the Old Testament.

After her birth and before the Annunciation, the only form of mediation Mary could exercise was that of intercessory prayer. And her prayers must have been very effective in hastening the coming of the promised Messiah. With the Annunciation her role as Mediatrix began in reality: first by consenting to be the mother of Jesus so that it is through her that we receive Jesus who is the source of all grace. Still more is Mary our Mediatrix on Calvary where she was one with Jesus as his spouse in giving her consent and acceptance to his saving sacrifice in the name of all mankind.

After Pentecost and before her departure from this life, it would appear that her active mediation was again limited to intercessory prayer for the welfare of the early Church.

Only after her Assumption into heaven does she now exercise her role as Mediatrix in all its fullness without any limitations. And this will continue until the number of the elect are complete at the end of time.

After the general resurrection her mediation in heaven will consist in receiving from Jesus and passing on to all her children all the joys of heaven. As a Queen receives everything from her spouse, the king, Mary will mediate all the riches of God to the blessed, then united as one happy family. For what, she will be to us beyond that, we can only say: "The eye has not seen nor the ear heard nor has it entered into the mind of man to conceive what God has prepared for those who love him." (1 Cor. 2:9)

PART II

THE LIFE OF MARY

MARY: GOD'S SUPREME MASTERPIECE

INTRODUCTION

In the first part of this book, I considered Mary in the light of what we can know of her through the principles of reason and faith. Here in this second part, I would like to consider the historical life of Mary in the light of these principles. Looking at her life in this way will help us see her as a model and inspiration of how we should live our own lives with God and for God. Although Mary's life really begins with her conception and birth, still, because of her intimate association with Jesus, our Savior, we find her foreshadowed and prefigured in many texts of Scripture.

Division of subject matter: In this second part, I would like to consider first how Mary has been prophesied and foreshadowed in both the Old Testament and in the New Testament. I will then consider Mary in the different stages of her life from her birth to her death and glorification.

CHAPTER I

MARY AS PROPHESIED AND FORESEEN IN SCRIPTURE

A) IN THE OLD TESTAMENT

Many texts of the Old Testament, when understood in the light of events in the New Testament, are clearly seen as prefiguring these later events and the persons involved in them. Thus we find Mary foreshadowed at the very beginning of Genesis in contrast to Eve. There we see it is Mary's offspring, Jesus, who will crush the head of Satan. God says to Satan, "I will make you enemies of each other: you and the woman, your offspring and her offspring. It will crush your head and you will strike its heel." (Gen. 3:15)

In Isaiah we see God answering Ahaz, "The Lord himself, therefore, will give you a sign. It is this: the maiden is with child and will soon give birth to a son whom she will call Emmanuel." (Is. 7:14) Mary is also seen as belonging to God's poor ones: the Anawim, who, in their need and weakness, put all their trust in God and not in man. Thus the Psalmist cries, to God, "Rise Yahweh, God, raise your hand, do not forget the poor...the luckless man commits himself to you: the orphan's certain help." (Ps. 10:12-14) These poor ones praise God and rejoice in him as their savior, "Sing to Yahweh, for he has delivered the soul of the needy from the hands of evil men." (Jer. 20:13) That Mary considered herself one of God's Anawim, is seen in her Magnificat. "He has looked upon his lowly handmaid; ... he has routed the proud of heart ... he has come to the help of Israel his servant, mindful of his mercy." (Lk. 1:48-54)

In the book of Judith, Mary is seen prefigured as "The most exalted daughter of Sion, the glory of Jerusalem, the joy of Israel and the highest honor of our race." (Jdt. 15:9) In the book of Esther, Mary is seen as taking her life in her hands for the salvation of her people. "My Lord. come to my help, for I am alone and have no helper but you, and I am about to take my life in my hands." (Est. C:14)

Many texts in the Wisdom books of the Bible have been applied to Mary by the Fathers of the Church, especially those that personify Wisdom. "God created me from the beginning before the oldest of his works, from everlasting I was firmly set." (Prov. 8:22) "Many daughters gather together riches; you have surpassed them all." (Prov. 31:29) Mary is seen as that singular and unique one, "One is my dove, my perfect one is but one." (Cant. 6:9) And again, "As a lily among thorns, so is my love among the daughters." (Cant. 2:2) "I am the mother of fair love and of fear and of knowledge and holy hope." (Eccl. 24:24)

B) IN THE NEW TESTAMENT

In the New Testament Mary is the subject of prophecies regarding the final accomplishment of our salvation. She is the bride of Christ, to be identified with the Church as found in St. Paul's letter to the Ephesians. There he speaks of the Church as being "Glorious and without spot or wrinkle, but holy and faultless." (Eph. 5:27) Only Mary is "without spot or wrinkle." Hence, what St. Paul says of the Church applies to Mary who is identified with the Church as its perfect model and exemplar, whom the faithful should seek to imitate.

In the book of Revelation, Chapter 12, we find Mary identified with the Church as "The woman adorned with the sun, standing on the moon, with twelve stars on her head as a crown ... in the act of giving birth." And like the Church, she is hated by Satan who seeks to destroy her child. But she and God's Church are protected from the hatred of Satan, who goes in pursuit of her children: the faithful whom he seeks to destroy. In the end Mary and the Church are to be victorious, but not without much suffering and persecution.

From these prophecies in the New Testament, we see that just as Mary is to be intimately united with Jesus at his coming in the Incarnation and in the work of his saving death on Calvary, so she is to be united with him in his Mystical Body, the Church, through the dispensing of his saving grace to all mankind down the ages to the end of time.

MARY: GOD'S SUPREME MASTERPIECE

CHAPTER II

MARY'S BIRTH AND EARLY LIFE

A) MARY'S CONCEPTION AND BIRTH

In the physical order, Mary's conception and birth were no different from that of every other human being. Only in the spiritual gifts of her soul was Mary exceptional. She alone, from the first moment of her conception was freed from the stain of original sin and most of its consequences.

Whether Joachim and Anne were the names of her parents we cannot know for sure, but they must have been exceptionally holy to be chosen to be the parents of such a child. It is generally thought that Anne was barren and that she conceived Mary through a special promise from God as were Isaac, Samuel, and John the Baptist. That may or may not be true. It is very likely that Mary was the only child of her parents: as a treasure of unique value she was more than sufficient to enrich their lives. Then too, if Anne had other children, the contrast between them and Mary, because of her special spiritual gifts and graces, would have been so great as to have created problems in the family.

B) MARY'S EARLY CHILDHOOD

In her early childhood, Mary must have been very precocious with a child-like simplicity, intelligence and goodness that were exceptional. Because she was without the effects of original sin she did not experience the concupiscence of the flesh. Her emotions were wholly under the control of her will and her mind was clear and unhampered in any way. Hence, her concept of God, as her creator and herself as his creature, must have established her in a deep enduring humility. Being possessed by the Holy Spirit, all her actions were guided by his inspirations. Also, being deeply conscious of her dependence on God and her duty of fulfilling his will, her docility to the guidance of the Holy Spirit was always complete and perfect. It is difficult for us to imagine the beauty and harmony of Mary's character and the perfect balance she must have revealed in all her actions.

Whether Mary was presented to God in the temple, as was Samuel by his mother, we have no way of knowing for certain. But we can be sure that at a very early age Mary consecrated her whole life to God by the total gift of herself, such as religious do when they make their profession. In this she is a perfect model for religious. When the Church celebrates the feast of Mary's Presentation it is this total gift of herself to God that is celebrated more than the historical way in which she expressed it.

C) MARY'S ADOLESCENT YEARS

As Mary's conscious mind developed, God must have been at the center of her thoughts and the one great object of her love. As she came to learn more about God and his great love, her precocious mind was quick to perceive God's special love for her people and indeed for all mankind. Externally her life must have been much like that of other young girls of those days, although her inner union with God was surely exceptional. She would have found great delight in the Scriptures and in the religious feasts of her people. While she helped with the work around the house and associated and played with the children of the neighborhood, she did so with a singular goodness and thoughtful charity.

Did her exceptional goodness become a source of suffering for Mary? Did God allow her to be persecuted through the envy of others. I remember a writer who suggested that Mary may have been referring to such a trial in her early life wherein her Magnificat, she says that, "God has looked upon the humiliation of his handmaid." Such a trial was not impossible. As Jesus was to say, "If the world hates you, remember that it hated me before you. If you belonged to the world, the world would love you, but because you do not belong to the world, therefore the world hates you." (Jn. 15:18)

D) MARY'S MAIDENHOOD AND MARRIAGE

While Mary certainly received greater and more abundant graces than any of the saints, that does not mean she was accustomed to mystical experiences and visions. The Bible records only one such vision granted to Mary: the Annunciation. Mary lived a life of faith, fruitful in works of hope and love much as is expected from all of us. If she was to be a model for all her children, she had to live the ordinary life of a woman in her day as Jesus himself did until he began his public ministry.

All the glory and beauty of Mary was within, not in external marvels and miraculous events. Her faith was so strong that God and the spiritual world were evident realities to her. Therefore, living with God in faith was the most powerful force in her life. She perceived God's goodness and greatness with such clarity that her whole life was centered in adoration, obedience, trusting abandonment and love. If consecrated religious, by knowing and loving God, are moved to dedicate their whole lives to his service through the evangelical vows, that was far more true of Mary.

Hence the question: "Did Mary make a vow of virginity or a resolve equal to such a vow?" The idea of choosing virginity as a way of life was certainly not in conformity with the customs of her people where marriage and motherhood were looked upon as the greatest glory for a woman. Only through the guidance of the Holy Spirit could Mary have come to recognize the supreme good of giving to God alone her undivided and intimate love through the renunciation of marriage. She was given to recognize and embrace this Christian value before it had been revealed to the world through Christ himself.

That Mary actually made such a vow or resolve of virginity seems quite certain. We have no other way of explaining her reply to the angel at the Annunciation, "How can this come about since I know not man." (Lk. 1:34) Since she was betrothed, the normal meaning of the angel's message would be that, once the marriage was consummated, she would conceive the promised child. That Mary did not take it that way, shows that she must have committed herself to remaining a virgin and that she still felt that to be God's will for her.

In the light of this we may wonder how it came about that her marriage with Joseph had been arranged in the first place. Was the marriage forced upon her by her parents or, since they may have been dead, by her relatives? For a mature girl to remain unmarried was certainly contrary to the belief of her people. How Joseph was chosen and accepted, we have no way of knowing. But we can be sure it was through a special arrangement of God's divine providence and that God had prepared Joseph for his exceptional mission. Knowing the sanctity Joseph must have had to be chosen by God as the spouse of Mary and the foster father of his divine Son and, knowing Mary's perfect sincerity and integrity, they must have come to some agreement, before the betrothal, on the matter of Mary's virginity.

It is very likely that Joseph agreed with Mary's resolve to remain a virgin and that he even freely chose to make a similar vow. Seeing that many Christian saints have been moved to consecrate their virginity to God, surely God would have given Joseph an even greater grace considering his exalted place in the mystery of the incarnation. We cannot over-estimate the holiness and virtue of Joseph, for he must have excelled all other saints after Mary herself. Since the intimate union which bound Mary and Joseph together was wholly spiritual, it must have been deeper and more total than that found in any other human marriage. We can be sure that Mary and Joseph deeply loved one another and found a mutual support therein, but their love for one another was entirely centered in their love for God.

CHAPTER III

MARY'S PLACE IN THE INCARNATION

The great glory of Israel was that she was to have the privilege of being the people through whom the savior of mankind was to come into the world. Hence, Israel looked forward to that coming with great longing as the crowning event in her history, whereby she would become a glory and a blessing to all the nations of the earth. Mary certainly shared this longing of her people and prayed for its speedily fulfillment.

But there was no clear understanding of how the coming Messiah was to fulfill his task of salvation. It was more generally thought that it would be some kind of political victory which would make Israel the greatest nation of earth, and all other nations would find their blessings by submitting to, and serving Israel. Did Mary share this view? What was her understanding of the Messiah and the nature of his mission? That is what I would like to consider first in this chapter before examining Mary's place in all the events dealing with the Incarnation, from the Annunciation to the end of Christ's hidden life.

A) MARY'S STATE OF MIND AT
THE TIME OF THE INCARNATION

Mary as a child of her people shared in their history, their knowledge and experience of God, and looked forward with them to the final glory that the promised Messiah was to inaugurate. She was well versed in the Scriptures and, no doubt, had a better understanding of their message than all the doctors of the law, because of her special gifts from God. However, her knowledge was limited, for we are told that she did not understand certain words and events, and that she kept these things in mind and pondering them in her heart. Mary was a pilgrim like ourselves and therefore she had to live by faith and not by vision. Her mortal life was a continual growth in knowing and loving like all other men and women.

What then was Mary's knowledge concerning the Messiah? She knew that he would be a member of our human race, a new lawgiver like Moses, raised up from his people. She could not have known that he would be a divine person taking upon himself our human nature. That was something completely foreign to the Jewish understanding of God. God could not be seen by man without dying, and God could not be depicted by any visible form. For Mary to have known Jesus as being the Son of God would have required a knowledge of the Trinity, a knowledge that cannot be found explicitly in the Old Testament and which would appear as wholly contrary to the Jewish belief in the oneness of God. No doubt God could have given Mary a special revelation concerning the divinity of Jesus, but there is no evidence that he did so. Otherwise she would have understood his reply when they found him in the temple, which we ourselves now easily understand, knowing that he is the Son of God.

What was Mary's concept of the mission of the Messiah? I am sure she had a more spiritual view than her contemporaries, especially the leaders of her people who expected a political Messiah. That she was given to recognize the special value of virginity consecrated to God would indicate that she saw spiritual values as far more important than any natural or political values. Did she foresee that the Messiah would have to suffer: that those words of Isaiah (chapter 50) about the suffering servant applied to the Messiah? These words of Isaiah were not generally believed to apply to the

Messiah by the Jews, and the apostles certainly did not imagine them as applying to Jesus. Even if Mary did not see them as applying to Jesus, she could have had some presentiment of his coming suffering, knowing that he was to save his people from their sins and that sacrifice had an important place in the worship of God. What the nature of his sufferings would be she could not have known with any clarity, but one things she would have been certain about is that the Messiah would triumph in the end.

As Moses had written, Mary certainly knew that the Messiah would be born a member of her people. But did she foresee or even desire the possibility of being his mother? I think we can say that she did not. She even seems to have willingly excluded that possibility by her vow or resolve of virginity. If there was a longing among Jewish maidens to be the mother of the Messiah, Mary did not share that ambition. Her insight into the value of virginity outweighed such a desire and also her deep humility would not have allowed her to entertain the thought of it. But it was just that humility and her total love for God as expressed in her vow of virginity that moved God to choose her, from all others to be the mother of his Messiah.

While Mary unknowingly prepared herself to be the mother of the Messiah, her prayers and ardent longing for his coming, united with those of her people and the prophets of old, surely helped to hasten that day. All was now in readiness for God to initiate the stupendous work of our redemption through the sending of his divine Son as a member of our human race.

B) THE ANNUNCIATION AND ASSOCIATED EVENTS

l. The Annunciation: "When the appointed time came, God sent his Son, born of a woman, born a subject of the law to redeem the subjects of the law and to enable us to be adopted as sons." (Gal. 4:4-5) "The angel Gabriel was sent by God... to a virgin betrothed to a man name Joseph of the house of David and the virgin's name was Mary." (Lk. 1:27) On coming before her, the angel greeted Mary with joy and reverence, "Rejoice so highly favored, the Lord is with you." Mary was troubled over the angel's greeting, but he said to her, "Do not be afraid for you have won God's favor. Listen, you are to conceive and bear a son and you must name him Jesus.

He will be great and will be called the Son of the Most High; the Lord God will give him the throne of David and he will rule over the house of Jacob forever." (Lk. 1:28-32)

Mary could not mistake the message; she was asked to be the mother of the long awaited Messiah. She, who in her humility, never dreamed of such an honor, now finds it being offered to her. But what about her vow of virginity? Hence her question, "How can this come about since I am a virgin?" To this the angel replies, "The Holy Spirit will come upon you and the power of the Most High will cover you with its shadow and so the child will be holy and will be called the Son of God." (Lk. 1: 35) It will be a work of God alone: she will become a mother by the power of God and not by man. Although the angel did not say the child would be God, neither did his words exclude it. That is the message; what is Mary's reply? Always humble and docile to God's will she could only answer, "I am the handmaid of the Lord, let what you have said be done to me." (Lk. 1: 38)

Here we have God asking the consent of his creature. God, in dealing with his free creatures, always respects their freedom, never forcing his supernatural will and gifts upon them. Mary's consent was so essential to God's plan for our salvation that, had Mary not given it, our redemption would never have gone forward. Of course, God had foreknowledge that Mary would give her consent, but that did not lessen the merit and freedom of Mary's consent. God is the source of every gift, but he has willed that, with regard to the supernatural gift of his divine friendship, our consent is absolutely necessary. He cannot and will not force his friendship upon us, for that is contrary to the very nature of friendship.

After the angel had gone, what thoughts, what emotions, filled the heart of Mary: How humble she must have felt before the greatness and condescension of God; how full of joy and gratitude, seeing how he passes over the great and mighty to choose the poor and weak. It was at this moment that those sentiments took root in Mary's heart to which she would later give expression in her Magnificat. She marveled at how God chose the poor and the weak in preference to the rich and mighty, so contrary to man's way of evaluating things. She marvels at the mercy of God in faithfully fulfilling the promise he made to Abraham and his descendants so many centuries before.

If Mary here seems to have taken her inspiration from the song of Anna, it is only because both had experienced similar acts of God's goodness and love for the poor and lowly. That too is why those individuals who have had a similar experience of God's merciful love, find the words of Mary's Magnificat re-echoing in their own hearts.

2. Place of Joseph in the Incarnation: Did Mary have anyone with whom she could share the joy and wonder that filled her heart? A general opinion seems to be that Mary kept everything to herself and that she did not even tell Joseph. I simply cannot believe that. If Joseph was holy enough to be chosen by God to be the husband of Mary and the foster father of his divine Son and, if he was so akin to Mary in spirit as to share her love for virginity, and if Mary, as his future wife, was most perfect in spousal love, sharing everything with her beloved and confiding in his loving goodness, then Mary would have been less than perfect had she not shared this event with Joseph. Indeed, Joseph had a right, as her future husband, to be fully informed of such a serious development in their mutual relationship. Nor did Mary's humility stand in the way, as some seem to think. A truly humble person does not have to hide the secret gifts of the king, as they say, for fear of pride. Mary saw her own nothingness so clearly that her only desire was to proclaim the goodness and greatness of the Lord without a thought for herself.

On hearing Mary's account Joseph must have truly rejoiced with Mary in what the Lord had done to her, but it also created a problem for himself. It was not that he disbelieved Mary's account and still less her virtue. It was his own humility that took fright: "Who was he to intrude into the life of one whom God had taken to himself in such an intimate way." Did Joseph share his problem with Mary? I would think that he did, and it must have become a source of mutual anguish for both of them. After careful thought and prayer, Joseph decided that the best thing for him to do would be to put Mary aside in an informal way without any publicity so as to cause the least possible suspicion. It was then that God came to the rescue. The angel appeared to Joseph in a dream and reassured him not to fear taking Mary as his wife just because she had conceived what was in her by the Holy Spirit.

Once Joseph knew the divine will he did not hesitate to take Mary into his home as his wife.

Marriage of Joseph and Mary: When did the marriage between Joseph and Mary take place? Normally the marriage followed only a few months after the agreement of betrothal. If Mary confided to Joseph the event of the Annunciation and Joseph's problem was settled within a week or so, it is very likely that their marriage took place before Mary's visit to her cousin Elizabeth. Knowing how prompt Joseph was in obeying the divine will, it is probable that he acted without delay as St. Matthew seems to indicate when he writes, "When Joseph woke up he did what the angel of the Lord told him to do; he took his wife to his home." (Mt. 1:24)

Knowing that God fully willed their marriage must have made it a very happy occasion for both Joseph and Mary. Their marriage was a true marriage even though it was never consummated in the flesh. Marriage is far more a union of minds and hearts than of bodies. If spouses lived that truth, there would not be so many divorces. Couples can always have the union of bodies, but when their union of mind and heart has died, they no longer have any desire for the union of bodies.

Since Joseph and Mary were most perfectly united in mind and heart, and indeed in a union wholly centered in their mutual love for God, we cannot imagine a more perfect marriage. It must have been somewhat like the friendships between some of the saints of the opposite sex: as St. Francis De Sales and St. Jean De Chantal, for example, only more intimate. Mary and Joseph saw each other as God's most precious gift to them and they found a wonderful mutual support in one another. Mary found great strength and security in the loving care of Joseph, and joyfully submitted to him in loving trust and abandonment. And Joseph found great comfort and self-assurance in Mary's tender love and esteem.

We will never fully understand the spiritual beauty and perfection of their married life, but we can be sure that no other human marriage will ever excel it. Their union must have been an earthly likeness to the union of loving friendship that will exist among the blessed in heaven. There all will be united in a mutual love for one another that is wholly centered in God without the carnal aspects of marriage, for then we will be like the angels in heaven.

3. The Visitation: At the Annunciation the angel told Mary about her cousin Elizabeth, that she, who had been barren, was now six months pregnant. Luke tells us that Mary set out at that time as quickly as she could to visit her cousin. (Lk. 1:39) Mary was moved to make this visit, certainly in order to congratulate and rejoice with Elizabeth in the great favor the Lord had given her, but also to offer her the help she would need when the child was born, especially seeing that Elizabeth was advanced in years. In the Annunciation we see Mary's perfect docility in accepting the will of God in her life; here in the visitation we see her perfect generosity in fully corresponding with what her acceptance of God's will required of her.

Who accompanied Mary on this journey? Surely a young maiden could not have made such a trip by herself in those days. The most likely one to accompany her would have been Joseph. If their marriage had just taken place, as I have suggested, this trip would have been somewhat like a honeymoon of today. The short delay of a week or two required for the marriage would have fitted in quite well with the time table given us by St. Luke. Since Elizabeth was six months pregnant at the time of the Annunciation and if Mary set out a few weeks later and stayed for three months, she would have returned home a few weeks after the birth of John the Baptist when Elizabeth could now take care of things herself. Certainly, if Joseph did not accompany Mary, we have no way of knowing who else might have done so.

Mary's only motive may have been to congratulate and help Elizabeth, but God, in his providence, had other plans in view. With Mary's greeting God enlightened Elizabeth concerning the divine motherhood of Mary and at the same time the child in Elizabeth's womb sensed the gift of God's grace coming to him from Jesus through Mary and leapt for joy. A tradition has it that Mary's greeting was the occasion for John the Baptist to be cleansed from original sin. Here God was using Mary as an instrument of his grace to others, and that is why the feast of the Visitation is considered as a manifestation of Mary's role as Mediatrix of all graces.

Mary may not have had any intention of mentioning to Elizabeth her own motherhood, but God willed to inspire Elizabeth with that knowledge. He also moved Elizabeth to proclaim Mary blessed, because of her great faith, and also to thank Mary for the honor of being visited by the mother of her Lord. These words stirred up in Mary's heart all the emotions she had experienced at the time of the Annunciation and she was moved to give expression to them in her beautiful Magnificat.

Since Mary remained with Elizabeth for about three months, she was certainly present at the birth of John the Baptist and experienced the marvels God displayed on that occasion. All these happenings must have given Mary much food for thought concerning the ways of God and about what the future was to hold in store for her and the child she was carrying in her own womb.

After their marriage and the Visitation, Mary and Joseph set up house in Nazareth awaiting the birth of Mary's child. What was the life of Mary and Joseph like at this time? Surely they found a wonderful mutual support in one another centered in God and directed to God. What were their thoughts and conversations concerning the recent events they had experienced? They clearly saw the hand of God in all these happenings and they knew that for the future, they must leave everything to God, in loving trust and abandonment.

Even though Mary did not know that her child was God, she knew he was the Messiah and therefore one greater than Moses and any of the prophets. Hence, she must have felt very close to God by reason of her child who was to be the savior of her people and of all mankind, and who was to reign on the throne of David forever. Mary experienced in her heart all the glorious expectations of the prophets and her nation and, indeed, of the whole world.

1. The Birth of Jesus: As Mary's time drew near and she was preparing for the birth of her child, divine providence began its hidden arrangements of events. Ceasar ordered a census to be taken of the world. Because Joseph was of the house of David, he was obliged to go to Bethlehem to be registered with his family. Complying with that decree upset the plans of Mary and Joseph and entailed many hardships, forcing them to put everything into the hands of God's loving providence. Did they wonder why God was doing this to them? We ourselves can now see in hindsight how wonderful and divine were all God's arrangements, but Mary and Joseph had to accept it on faith.

In this way the prophecy that the Messiah was to be born at Bethlehem would be fulfilled. Also revealed, was God's preference for the poor and the suffering, for the displaced persons and for all those rejected by the rich and great: all those who are forced to rely in God's loving, providential care. We see God's wonderful condescension in coming to share our human condition and how he chose to live the beatitudes himself before proclaiming them to the world.

It was through these arrangements that God gave us the most touching of all feasts: that of Christmas. No feast of the year touches the human heart like Christmas. That God should come into our world as a little child reveals a wisdom, and loving condescension that completely wins the human heart. No one can fail to love a little child; that is why God chose to come to us as a little one. We cannot help but see God's love therein and be moved to love him in return. Only God could have invented the reality of Christmas. With the psalmist we must say, "How wonderful are all your works 0 God, in wisdom you have made them all. (Ps. 103:24)

On arriving at Bethlehem Joseph and Mary could find no suitable place to stay, and not knowing anyone who could take them in, they ended up occupying a hillside stable, all alone with nature and its God. There in solitude and obscurity one of the most stupendous events in human history took place: God was born into our human race. God became man and lived among us; Mary gave birth to her divine child without loss of her virginity. While in prayerful union with God, her child left her womb and was found in Mary's arms, much as Jesus would later rise from the sealed tomb. Mary carefully and lovingly wrapped him in swaddling clothes and laid him in the manger so as to look down on him with wonder and loving admiration.

Suddenly the silence of the night was broken by the approach of shepherds coming to the cave. They came to see the newborn child, and told about an apparition of angels. An angel had appeared to them as they watched their flocks, and announced to them, "Today in the town of David a savior has been born to you, who is Christ the Lord, and you will find the baby wrapped in swaddling clothes and lying in a manger." (Lk. 2:11-12) They were more astonished when a great throng of the heavenly host appeared praising God and singing, "Glory to God in the highest heaven and peace to men who enjoy his favor." (Lk. 2:14)

Mary had not seen nor heard the angels; only the shepherds had, but Mary kept pondering their story in her heart. Hers was a life of faith. She must have wondered about who her child really was, his identity and his relationship to God. "Who is Jesus?" must have been the all absorbing quest of Mary's life, even as it should be also ours, although from a different perspective.

Later on, the Magi came from the East, led by a star, to pay homage to the newborn savior of the world. By that time, the Holy Family was in a home, since that is where the Magi found them. Here again, Mary must have marveled at the ways of God and pondered over what it all meant. The humble poor and the truly wise were the only ones who were given to recognize the coming of the world's savior.

Did the Magi come two years after the birth of Jesus: the time when they first saw the star, or did God make the star appear two years earlier than his actual birth so that, historically, they arrived shortly after the birth of Jesus? We have no way of knowing. They certainly arrived after the circumcision of Jesus and his presentation in the temple. It was right after their visit that Mary and Joseph had to flee with the child into Egypt.

2. Circumcision and Presentation: After the birth of Jesus a number of events followed that were semi-public: the Circumcision and the Presentation of Jesus in the temple, together with Mary's Purification. At the Circumcision, Jesus became incorporated into his people, shed his first blood and received the name of Jesus which had been given him by the angel. The Circumcision took place eight days after the birth of Jesus. By that time Mary and Joseph would be living in a house where the Magi found them. Surely Joseph would have done all he could to find a suitable shelter after the emergency of that first night.

Forty days after Christ's birth, Mary and Joseph went to Jerusalem to present Jesus to God in the temple, and Mary to receive the rite of purification. Every newborn male child in Israel belonged to God in a special way. When God freed Israel from Egypt he spared the first-born sons of the Israelites while the destroying angel killed all the first-born sons of the Egyptians. For that reason God made claim to every first-born son in Israel. Each one had to be offered to God in his temple and then redeemed at a price.

When Mary made this offering of her son to God, she must have united herself along with Jesus. How could she ever be separated from Jesus in giving Him to God? Did Mary recall those words of the psalmist, "Burnt offerings and sin offerings you did not want: then I said Behold I come, in the head of the book it is written of me that I should do your will O God," (Ps. 39:7-9)

At this time also Mary submitted to the rite of purification, required of every mother who gave birth to a child. Although Mary certainly needed no purification, she submitted to this law in humble obedience. She also made the offering required of the poor: two doves or two young pigeons, for that is all that Joseph could afford. It was in the midst of this ritual that Simeon and Anna appeared on the scene.

Simeon had been told by the Holy Spirit that he would not die before he had seen the Messiah of the Lord. Moved by the Holy Spirit, he came into the temple at this time and came up to Mary, took the child into his arms and blessed God for the privilege of resting his eyes on the Messiah. Now he could depart in peace, having seen the salvation God had prepared for all the nations. As Joseph and Mary stood there in wonderment, Simeon turned to Mary and said, "You see this child, he is destined for the fall and rise of many in Israel ... and a sword will pierce your own heart." (Lk. 2:34) Anna also came upon the scene at this time and began to praise God and tell all those who were looking forward to Israel's deliverance about the child.

When all was over and they departed from the temple, what thoughts must have gone through Mary's mind. The words of Simeon must have made her recall the words of Scripture about God's suffering servant and her joy became tinged with fear and anxiety. Mary's life, like our own, was to be mingled with joys and sorrows. We need both for our proper spiritual growth even as plants need sunshine and rainstorms to become mature and fruitful.

D) THE FLIGHT INTO EGYPT AND THE HIDDEN LIFE

It was only after these events that the visit of the Magi occurred: how soon we cannot really know. It could have been as long as two years or perhaps only a few weeks, depending on whether God made the star appear to the Magi before the time of Christ's birth or only at the same moment. If it was two years afterwards, we might wonder what was the relationship during that time between the Holy Family and their neighbors. Did the rumors arising from the shepherds and the happenings in the temple in Jerusalem become known to the people living with them?

1. The flight into Egypt: The visit of the Magi certainly changed all of this. After the Magi left, Joseph was warned by an angel in a dream to flee into Egypt because Herod would seek to destroy the child. Waking from his dream, Joseph left that very night for Egypt; he did not wait till dawn. What a shock for that little family. They were now persecuted refugees as so many others would be in the centuries to come. They were to experience the trials of being displaced persons, living in a foreign land among strangers. It was Mary's first fear for the well-being of her child and it must have made her recall the words of Simeon that her child would be a sign that is rejected. Did Mary hear about the massacre of the Holy Innocents while in exile? If she did, it must have been a source of deep sorrow to her and increased her fear of what the future had in store for her child. Although divine providence surely watched over them during their trip and exile, that did not lessen the suffering and the many difficulties they had to endure. Most likely the sale of the gifts the Magi had offered Jesus supplied them for their material needs at this time.

Why did God will that the Holy Family should be exiled in Egypt? One reason, which St. Matthew tells us, was to fulfill the prophecy, "I have called my Son out of Egypt." (Hos. 11:1) Of course these words of Hosea refer primarily to God's rescue of his people from their slavery in Egypt, but here Matthew sees them as referring to the Messiah. Another reason could have been to stop rumors about the identity of the Messiah arising from the shepherd's account, the events in Jerusalem at the presentation and from the coming of the Magi. God wanted the Messiah to remain unknown to the public until the moment of Christ's public ministry. No doubt that too is why God did not let Joseph settle his little family again in Judea or Bethlehem after his return from exile in Egypt. Being warned in his sleep, Joseph settled his family in Nazareth.

2. The Infancy accounts; are they historical: Permit me to make a little digression here concerning the historical reality of the infancy narratives in Matthew and Luke. I know that some scholars consider much of these accounts to be midrash, that is, a pious story with a spiritual lesson behind it. I find it hard to accept that. The accounts of Christ's infancy may not be historical in our modern literal sense of history, but the essential events contained therein are certainly historical facts.

If we are to accept the expressed intention of the New Testament writers themselves, we must believe that they were giving us historical facts even if not always in a precise historical form. St. Luke tells us that "Others had undertaken to draw up accounts of events that had taken place among them exactly as these were handed down to them by those who, from the beginning, were eye-witness and ministers of the word." (Lk. 1:1-4) He then goes on to say that, "Having carefully gone over the whole story himself from the beginning, he has decided to write an ordered account of the same events." Other writers of the New Testament attest to the same intention. St. John tells us that he vouches for the things he has written down and that his testimony is true. (Jn. 21:24) And in his first epistle he tells us that he is only writing about, "what he has seen with his own eyes and touched with his own hands." (1 Jn. 1:1) St. Peter in Acts says, "We cannot stop proclaiming what we have seen and heard." (Acts 4:20)

It is unreasonable to assume that the apostles and the early Christians did not ask Mary about the early life of Jesus and it is just as unreasonable to think that Mary, in her deep humility and self-forgetfulness, would not have readily revealed all the glorious deeds of God.

The apostles and early Christians were concerned only with the facts and what those facts meant for all mankind. They did not have to invent stories, for they had more than enough material in the historical events themselves. Since it is believed that Mary lived for many years after the Ascension, the apostles and the early Christians certainly had time to inquire from Mary about the early life of Jesus, and she would have had no reason to hold back anything.

3. The Hidden life: After the return from Egypt, the Holy Family made its home in Nazareth, a small town in Galilee. Here Jesus spent most of his life on earth, from perhaps the age of 6 to 30: some 24 years. All we are told about him during this time is that "He grew in wisdom and stature and in favor with God and man." (Lk. 2:52) Only one incident is recounted in the Gospel as having taken place during these years: the three day loss in the temple.

The life at Nazareth: The daily life of the Holy Family at Nazareth must have been much like that of other people in the town, but the peace and unity in love within their home was surely something very special. Apparently Joseph and Mary were the only or, at least, the principal teachers of Jesus. His education centered around the reading of Scripture, the history of their nation, and the meaning of their religious feasts. No doubt Jesus was a quick and eager learner and must have surprised Joseph and Mary with his questions and observations as he was to do later among the doctors of the law in the temple.

Jesus also helped with the household work and later, as he became older, he helped Joseph in his carpenter trade. The daily routine was punctuated by the weekly Sabbath and other celebrations of the religious feasts of their people which made everyone so conscious of God's providential love and care for their nation down the ages.

Like every mother, Mary must have watched her child grow and develop and she rejoiced at his every new accomplishment. But Mary and Joseph too, must have grown in their knowledge of Jesus by pondering on the many things he did and said. During this time the one predominant question in Mary's mind was the personal identity of Jesus and his spiritual relationship with God by reason of being the Messiah. He had to be someone very special: a greater than Moses and all the prophets of old. But in what that consisted, is what she sought to know more fully.

The three days loss: In the midst of these happy years occurred the three days loss in the temple. It gives us some insight into the Life and relationship that existed in the Holy Family. Being faithful Jews, Mary and Joseph went to Jerusalem for the Passover feast each year and Jesus went with them once he was old enough. However, when Jesus reached the age of twelve, at which age he became a legal adult and so legally free from the tutelage of his parents, something different happened. Jesus chose to stay behind in Jerusalem without telling his parents.

Knowing how parents grieve when their child is lost, we can understand something of the suffering Mary and Joseph experienced on this occasion. Only after three days of anxious searching did they find him in the temple. On finding him Mary's spontaneous question was, "My child why did you do this to us?" (Lk. 2:48) Mary's puzzlement was all the greater because Jesus had never done anything like this before. He was always so thoughtful and considerate. Hence his answer, "Did you not know that I must be about my Father's affairs?" (Lk. 2:49) took her by surprise, and she did not understand his answer. His words became another one of those things Mary was to keep in mind pondering on them in her heart.

In this event we see that Mary and Joseph were not over-possessive of Jesus. That they traveled a full day, believing that Jesus was in the caravan, showed that they trusted Jesus and were willing to let him have the freedom to be himself and mix with others. They were not over-controlling of him as some parents tend to be.

Here too we find Jesus, for the first time, speaking of God as his Father: "I must be about my Father's affairs." Since he was certainly not referring to Joseph, Mary puzzled about the meaning of this also. Jesus' reply must have been a reminder to Mary and Joseph that he had a mission to fulfill which would one day take precedence over family ties.

Maturing years of Jesus at Nazareth: After the three days loss, Luke tells us that Jesus went back with Mary and Joseph to Nazareth and lived under their authority, while Mary stored up all these things in her heart. Although Jesus was now an adult, he willed to remain under the authority of his parents. What a lesson of obedience for us. Jesus wills to live under obedience to his creature even though he is no longer obliged to do so even by reason of his humanity. However, being an adult, Jesus' relationship with Mary and Joseph now becomes more mature and more like that between equals. What must have been their conversations especially concerning Jesus' future. How much did Jesus tell them about his future mission? Certainly both Mary and Joseph knew Jesus was the Messiah, and so it is difficult to think that his special vocation did not come up in their conversations.

As Jesus became of age for marriage, there had to be some understanding about what he intended on this issue. With regard to his mission as the Messiah there is one thing he must have revealed to Mary, namely, that although she was to have no part in his public ministry, she would be united with him in the hour of his supreme triumph. That Mary was given this knowledge seems to he implied at the marriage feast at Cana when Jesus said to her, "My hour has not yet come." (Jn. 2:4) It is difficult to understand the meaning of these words if Mary had not been given to know that she would be united with him in his supreme hour of victory, and that; this was not the hour.

Death of Joseph: It appears that it was in this period, following Jesus' return to Nazareth, that Joseph died, for we have no mention of him at any time during Jesus' public life. There were good reasons for his death to occur in these years. Jesus was now capable of providing for Mary and having to support his widowed mother would have caused less reason for wondering why Jesus was not getting married at the normal age.

The death of Joseph must have been a great sorrow for both Mary and Jesus. They certainly loved Joseph with a very deep human affection as the best of fathers and husband. Although perfectly submissive to God's will in the matter, that did not lessen their grief, but enabled them to rise above it and turn it to spiritual growth as God intended.

For Joseph to have Jesus and Mary at his side during his dying hours was certainly a great comfort and support to him. It is because of this privilege that Joseph is considered the patron of a happy death. We pray that he might win for us the same grace of having Jesus and Mary at our side when the time comes for us to pass from this life into eternity.

CHAPTER IV

MARY AND THE REDEMPTION

With the beginning of Jesus' public life a complete change took place both in the life of Mary and in the life of Jesus. The great work for which everything so far had been preparing him, was now to begin: the salvation of the world, the salvation of all mankind. If Mary had such an important place in the preparation, she is to have a still greater place in the work itself. Indeed, she will be united with Jesus as his other self, completing him in his human nature as social and also as the head and leader of a new divinized mankind. Jesus is to be the active agent of our redemption, the bridegroom, and Mary is to be the passive agent, consenting and accepting it as his bride in our place.

In this chapter I would like to consider Mary's relationship with Jesus during his public life, and her part with Jesus in the actual work of our redemption. I will also consider Mary's relationship with Jesus in the events of his Resurrection and Ascension.

A) MARY DURING CHRIST'S PUBLIC LIFE

We may wonder, when the time came for Jesus to begin his public life, how he took his departure from Mary. Since he was the only support of his widowed mother, he had to make some arrangement for her during the time of his ministry. From both (Mt. 4:13) and

(Jn. 2: 12) we see that Jesus left Nazareth with his mother and made his home in Capernaum. Most likely he had some relatives there with whom he could leave her. Since he planned to make that city a kind of home base, he could see her from time to time whenever he returned there. It would also appear that his separation from her was not complete at first, but only after Cana when the apostles became his habitual companions. Only twice is Mary mentioned in the public life of Jesus: at Cana and one time when she was with some relatives asking to see Jesus.

Mary at Cana: At Cana it is thought that Mary prompted Jesus to begin his public ministry by asking him to work his first miracle: the sign that moved his disciples to believe in him. The marriage at Cana must have been that of some relative or family friend since Mary and also Jesus with his disciples were invited. It is very likely that Mary herself had helped in the preparation, and hence, kept an eye upon the needs of the occasion as the celebration progressed That is why she was quick to see that the wine was running low and brought the matter to the attention of Jesus.

What did Mary expect Jesus to do? Did she expect a miracle or, knowing that Jesus was good at solving difficult situations, did she simply trust that he would find a remedy? From Jesus' reply, "Woman, why turn to me? My hour has not yet come," it would appear that she was thinking of her share in Jesus' Messianic work and so was asking him to begin it by working this first miracle. Hence, she did not take Jesus' reply as a refusal to help, but only as telling her this was not the hour when she would be united with him in his saving work. Therefore she said to the servants, "Do whatever he tells you." They did so, and Jesus gave the first sign of his divine mission and his disciples found faith in him.

Mary knew Jesus was the Messiah and that he was now entering upon his mission which would be evidenced by miracles. That miracles would reveal the Messiah Jesus himself indicated when, in his reply to the disciples of John the Baptist who were asking whether he was the Messiah or not, Jesus replied, "Go back and tell John what you have seen, the blind see, the lame walk, the lepers are cleansed, the deaf hear and the dead are raised to life." (Lk. 7:22) These were the signs Isaiah said would herald the coming of God. (Isa. 35:5-6)

The miracle at Cana was Christ's first miracle and perhaps not just the first of his public ministry, but of his whole life. Jesus did not work miracles for personal reasons, as is evident when the devil tempted him to change stones into bread. We have no account of Jesus working miracles before this or any reason to think he did so. It is very likely that, Mary, in her longing for Jesus to inaugurate his Messianic mission, was inspired, by her great faith and trust in Jesus, to ask him to begin his Messianic work by performing this first miracle. And how could Jesus refuse her, seeing that he could never refuse anyone who came to him for help with faith and confidence. Thus Jesus willed that Mary should be the one who would start him on his Messianic mission even as she was responsible for many other beginnings in his life.

Mary with her relatives: The only other time Mary appeared in the public life of Jesus was when she, with other relatives, were standing outside a house asking to see Jesus. Jesus used the occasion to teach his disciples an important lesson, "Who is my mother, who are my brothers? and pointing towards his disciples he said, "Here are my mother and brothers. Anyone who does the will of my Father in heaven he is my brother and sister and mother." (Mk. 3:33-35) Jesus is here telling us that it is not a physical relationship with Jesus that is all important, but a spiritual and moral relationship with him based on faith and love. However, since no one was ever more perfectly united with Jesus in doing the will of God through faith and love than Mary, Jesus is not here disparaging his mother but indicating her greatest title to glory.

After this event Mary no longer appears openly in the Gospel account. We do not even hear of her being among the group of women who often accompanied Jesus on his travels, though it is quite possible. We can be sure that Mary was always united with Jesus in spirit and in prayer, and that she followed the events of his ministry through the information given her by others and, no doubt also, from Jesus himself when he came back to Capernaum in the course of his many journeys. What they spoke about on those visits we would love to know, but that will have to wait until we get to heaven.

As opposition to Jesus began to stiffen, Mary must have come to suspect the outcome, especially if she had been told about Jesus' prediction of his future suffering at the hands of the Jewish leaders. I doubt that she was told of this seeing that the apostles themselves did not know what to make of it. But even without knowing this, the words of Simeon about Jesus being destined for the fall and for the rising of many in Israel, and a sign that is to be rejected, must have made her suspect that her own soul would be pierced by the sword of sorrow on account of her son's fate.

B) MARY'S PART IN THE WORK OF OUR REDEMPTION

1. The last supper: Christ's redemptive hour began with the Last Supper. It was also the hour of darkness, the hour of the great conflict between good and evil, between God's infinite love and rebellious human pride. Although it appears that Mary was not present at the last supper, we can be sure that she was united with Jesus in spirit: in a union of love and compassion more intimate than that which was to be shared by many mystics in the future.

Mary must have sensed that the end was near when she received the news that the Jewish leaders had ordered Jesus' arrest and that they should be informed of his whereabouts. Her heart must have bled with a cruel anticipation, not too unlike Jesus' own agony in the garden. All that she knew from Scripture about the suffering servant must have loomed before her eyes. "He was pierced for our faults, crushed for our sins; on him lies a punishment that brings us peace." (Isa. 53:5) "If he offers his life in atonement he will see his heirs, he will have a long life." (Isa. 53:10) Other texts also must have come to her mind, "Sacrifice and oblations you would not, then I said I am here to do your will." (Ps. 39:7) "I am a worm and no man, the laughing stock of the people." (Ps. 21:7) When the fleeing apostles, therefore brought her news of Jesus' arrest, she knew that this was his hour, the hour he had referred to at Cana, when she would be united with him.

How close Mary was physically to the various events of Jesus' passion we are not told. Christian piety has her meeting Jesus while carrying his cross on his way to Calvary. This may well have taken place. Mary may have been present also on the outskirts of the crowd with the other women who had followed Jesus, witnessing the proceeding of his trial. How painful to hear her own people prefer Barabbas to Jesus and cry for the death of her son by crucifixion. On the way to Calvary did she hear remarks such as, "Well, they have finally found out that he is a fake, that he is just another false teacher who is trying to deceive the people." It is difficult to comprehend the depths of anguish in Mary's heart, not only over the sufferings of her son Jesus, but also over the rejection of him by his own people. Knowing that Jesus was the Messiah, how difficult it must have been even for Mary to understand God's way of dealing with Jesus. She too must have had her moment when she prayed, "O God if it be possible let this chalice pass from me and from Jesus, yet not as I will but as you will."

2. Mary on Calvary: We know for certain, and it is St. John who tells us: Mary was present on Calvary standing, not fainting, near the cross of Jesus. But who can plumb the depths of her sorrow? Perhaps only a mother who has had a child disappear, and later found to have been tortured and killed, can know something of her anguish. But how much greater would that mother's anguish be were she actually present at her child's suffering, yet powerless to stop it or even give her child any help or comfort. From a human point of view such a comparison may give us some idea of Mary's suffering on Calvary. But Mary was not merely a spectator on Calvary, she was deeply involved in the Mystery that was being enacted.

Mary saw beyond the physical suffering of Calvary to the spiritual reality: that of sacrifice, and she was a participator in that sacrifice. Jesus was the Paschal Lamb sacrificing himself to free his people from their sins. Mary was united with him as his bride whom he had taken to himself. Mary stood at the foot of the cross in the place of all mankind, consenting, accepting and uniting herself with Jesus in his total gift of himself to his Father. As Jesus was offering himself as priest and victim to God in sacrifice, Mary was offering herself with Jesus as his bride, the new Eve, consenting and accepting his sacrifice in the name of all mankind.

Mankind in Mary: In Mary, all mankind, the sinful bride Jesus had taken to himself, was united with Jesus in his redeeming sacrifice whereby Jesus removed God's displeasure with his bride. On Calvary, Mary was one with humankind, renounced sin and gave herself in total adherence to the divine will, thus enabling Jesus to make amends for mankind's sin against God. Jesus could now introduce his bride, all mankind, into the divine family of God as one with himself, sharing in all his own riches and privileges as being God's divine Son. Jesus' Father now becomes our Father and Jesus' God our God.

Mary's consent and cooperation given on Calvary was not given merely by words or an intention of the mind but by the actual gift or sacrifice of everything more dear to her than her own life: the immolation of her divine Son. Mary is truly our co-redeemer. Christ alone is our savior, for he alone laid down his life in sacrifice, but Mary had a real place in that sacrifice even as Eve in our fall. As Eve is the mother of all who are born of Adam, so Mary is the mother of all the children who are born by baptism into the divine life of the new Adam, Jesus. And this, her motherhood was proclaimed by Jesus from the cross when, seeing his disciple John, he said to Mary, "Woman this is your son," and to John, "This is your mother." (Jn. 19:26-27)

What Mary did in our place on Calvary we must now do in our own name when we assist at the same sacrifice made present on our altars at Mass. We must offer Jesus, and ourselves with him, as our own most precious gift to God in sacrifice. God cannot give us his divine life of friendship without our free acceptance. Therefore, the more perfectly we accept Christ's sacrifice, in our own name, by uniting ourselves with Jesus in faith and trust, in likeness to Mary, the more fully will we share, first in Mary's perfect union with Jesus in human friendship, and then with Jesus in his perfect union with his Father in divine friendship.

3. Mary's highest act of love: On Calvary Mary's love or charity reached the highest peak possible to a creature of God. There is no greater love for a man than to lay down his life for his friend, yet Mary, in her love for God, sacrificed something dearer to her than her own life: the sacrifice of Jesus. Jesus in his humanity reached his highest peak of human charity when, on Calvary, he gave himself as man to his Father in the very act of love whereby, in the life of the Trinity, he gives himself eternally, as God, to the Father in the Holy Spirit. In much the same way Mary reached her highest possible peak of charity when, united with Jesus in his total gift of love for his Father, she willingly renounced all her rights over her divine Son and freely offered him in perfect submission to the divine will.

St. Thomas Aquinas tells us that charity increases when we perform an act of charity more intense than any previous act. Now we cannot imagine how Mary could have had an occasion to perform a more intense act of charity in her subsequent life than the one she performed on Calvary. While Mary certainly increased in merit after Calvary, we cannot see how her charity could have increased by any more intense act. Hence, it would appear that Mary must have lived the rest of her life in that abiding state of charity she reached on Calvary. Perhaps only a mystic, who has reached the highest stage of mystical union with God, can give us some inkling of what Mary's life of union with God must have been after Calvary.

C) MARY AT THE RESURRECTION AND ASCENSION

After the death of Jesus what sorrow filled the heart of Mary. How alone she must have felt and what support she must have found in St. John at that moment, even though, she herself was a far greater support and source of courage to St. John.

1. Mary and the Resurrection: When Jesus was taken down from the cross, was he laid in the arms of Mary as depicted in Michelangelo's pieta? Most likely not because of the obligation to finish the burial before the setting of the sun. However, the pieta is a loving and pious expression of the Christian understanding and compassionate union with the heart of Mary in her supreme moment of loss and suffering.

Great as Mary's suffering was at that moment, she was never without hope. She knew that Jesus would be victorious in the end, that, like the suffering servant, "His soul's anguish over, he shall see the light and be content ... he will divide the spoils with the mighty for surrendering himself to death." (Isa. 53:11-12) That Jesus' triumph would consist in his rising from the dead, she may not have known unless the apostles had told her about Christ's prediction of his sufferings and resurrection. Unlike the apostles, Mary, so full of grace, would have readily understood its meaning.

After the burial of Jesus, John took Mary into his home. What did they share with one another? Mary surely shared some of her hopes with John. That is why John was the first of the apostles to believe in Jesus' resurrection on entering the empty tomb after Peter. He had been prepared for it by Mary. None of the other apostles believed in the resurrection until they had seen Jesus himself.

Necessity of the Resurrection: The resurrection of Jesus was necessary to prove that God had accepted the atoning sacrifice of

Jesus for the sins of mankind and as restoring us to God's divine friendship. The apostles were to be his official witnesses who were to proclaim this historical reality before the whole world. That is why only those apparitions, given mainly to the apostles and some of Christ's disciples, are mentioned in the Gospel. There is no mention of Jesus appearing to Mary, but we can be certain that he did. Indeed, Mary must have been the first to know the joy of Jesus' supreme victory. If Mary was so united with Jesus in his suffering of Calvary it was only right that she should share in his victory before all others. Being a dutiful son, it is impossible that Jesus would not have shared the joy of his triumphal resurrection with Mary before all others on that glorious Easter morning.

Sentiments in the heart of Mary: What sentiments must have filled the heart of Mary when she saw Jesus in all the glory and beauty of his risen body. If at the annunciation Mary was overwhelmed at seeing how God chose the lowly to exalt them above the great ones of this world, what must have been the emotions of her heart on seeing how God turned the greatest of sufferings into such a glorious and unimaginable victory. At the annunciation, Mary expressed the fullness of her heart in the words of her Magnificat. Perhaps at the resurrection those words of the psalmist reechoed in her soul, "I will tell of your name to my brethren and praise you where they are assembled ... you are my theme of praise in the great assembly. My soul shall live with him: my children serve him. They shall tell of the Lord to generations yet to come...these things the Lord has done." (Ps. 21:23-32)

If, during her life, Mary wondered about the mystery of suffering and evil, as we all do at one time or another, she must have seen the answer in the death and resurrection of Jesus. The heart of the two disciples on the road to Emmaus burned within them when Jesus explained from the Scriptures how it was necessary that the Christ should suffer and thus enter into his glory. Mary was surely given to see the meaning of these texts of Scripture far more clearly than these two disciples and her heart too must have burned with wonder at how God could bring forth so great a blessing; the salvation of all mankind, from so great an evil.

Christ's glorious resurrection, coming right after his apparent defeat, was surely a tremendous experience: a kind of turning point in the lives of Mary and the apostles. It was an experience similar to that found in the lives of many saintly souls when they come out of the suffering and darkness of the Night of the Senses and especially the Night of the Spirit as described by St. John of the Cross. From the very darkness and sufferings of their former days, which looked like the total destruction of everything they hoped for, God gave them the joy of seeing their own nothingness disappear in the light of his infinite goodness and unfailing love. They found such total confidence and security in God's infinite love and providential care, that they experienced a deep peace such as the world could never give, a peace which only comes from passing through death into the glory of God's divine love. It is a peace that comes from seeing suffering bud forth into the greatest of all blessings.

2. Mary discovers Christ's divinity: I like to think that what overwhelmed Mary most of all at the resurrection of Jesus is that, at that moment she was given to recognize that Jesus was truly God. During her whole life she had pondered on the identity of Jesus. She longed to know the reality of his personality from the many prophetic events and words she had experienced. Surely there was no more appropriate moment when all her ponderings should have burst into a moment of enlightenment than when she saw Jesus before her in all his risen glory. That vision created a whole new dimension in the life of Mary. It was like a new revelation of God's unfathomable love and condescension that overwhelmed her heart with joy and wonder. Her Son was actually God himself. She had been living with God all her life and did not know it. God deigned to be her child, to submit to her authority. What a marvel of self-giving and humility on God's part. She had been living in a human and loving relationship with God himself. O! what a vision was hers. All the events of the past took on a whole new meaning. For the rest of her life on earth she must have gone over all the past events in her life with Jesus, seeing them now in this new and marvelous light.

The first person with whom Mary must have shared her new discovery was St. John. How could she fail to speak to him about all she now knew of Jesus in the light of his resurrection. It was something that would occupy their thoughts for days and even years. Her discovery must have moved St. John to recall all those words of Jesus which implied his divinity, which he and the apostles never fully understood, especially his discourse after the Last Supper. No wonder John could recall so well all these words of Jesus years later when he wrote his Gospel. They were so fixed in his mind through his sharing them with Mary. While John told Mary about all the words of Jesus during his public life that implied his divinity, Mary must have told John about all the events, in the early life of Jesus, that implied the same. What a revelation for both of them, which they had to share with the apostles and they in their turn with all the early Christians.

But how did they understand the divinity of Jesus in the light of their Jewish belief in the unity of God? How did they come to recognize the Trinity? Was Mary given to understand this by a special revelation or did it come to light through her exchange with St. John who recalled the words of Jesus concerning his unity with the Father and the Holy Spirit? I think the latter was more likely the case. Now we can see why St. John was so strong in stressing the divinity of Jesus in his Gospel, and his unity with the Father and the Holy Spirit.

How Mary, the apostles and the early Christians understood the mystery of the Trinity, we have no way of knowing. The present explanation: that of three persons existing in one divine nature was given many years later by the Magisterium of the Church through the instrumentality of Greek philosophy, and definitively settled by the councils of Nicaea 325 and Constantinople 1,381.

3. The Ascension: We do not know how often Jesus showed himself to Mary after his resurrection. But we can be sure Mary heard about those apparitions that were given to the apostles and other disciples and perhaps she was present at some to them.

Although it is not mentioned that Mary was present at the Ascension, we can be sure that she was present. Jesus as a loving son would never have taken such a departure from his mother, a departure that was to last for many years, without saying good-bye in the most thoughtful way. It is very likely he informed her that he was going to leave her on earth for many years. Her new children, the member's of his Mystical Body, the Church, would stand in need of her motherly encouragement, example and prayers. And Mary, always perfectly submissive to the divine will, lovingly accepted to remain with us, her new children, even at the expense of being separated from Jesus in his physical presence.

The fact that, right after the Ascension, the apostles are said to have gone to the upper room to await the coming of the Holy Spirit and that Mary was with them, would imply that she had been with them just before on the Mount of Olives at his Ascension. While it must have been painful for Mary to see Jesus depart, she was happy for his sake, knowing that he would be united with his Father in eternal glory.

Mary also realized, as Jesus had told his apostles, "It is expedient that I go, otherwise the Holy Spirit will not come to you." (Jn. 16:7) Mankind must now live with Jesus present in the Spirit and no longer in the flesh and that is what Mary's life from now on would be: an example of how we must live with Jesus in the Spirit through faith. Like Mary our hearts must be with Jesus in heaven while our bodies are still on earth.

MARY: GOD'S SUPREME MASTERPIECE

CHAPTER V

MARY AT PENTECOST
AND IN THE CHURCH

After Christ's Ascension, another important change took place in Mary's life. She now became the contemplative in the fullest sense. She was indeed a contemplative all her life, but then she had never been without some duties and obligations of the active life. But now after Christ's ascension into heaven, her heart was entirely centered on heavenly things, as St. Paul tells us. "You must look for the things that are in heaven where Christ is seated at the right hand of God. Let your thoughts be on heavenly things, not on the things that are on the earth. Because you have died and now the life you live is hidden with Christ in God." (Col. 3:1-3) What St. Paul recommends to all Christians, Mary fulfilled in the highest possible degree. However, Mary was not aloof from the apostles and the early Christians even though her life was now wholly centered on Christ in heaven more than ever before. Now she no longer had any other pressing occupation but union with God in prayer.

Here in this chapter we will consider Mary's presence at Pentecost and her influence on the early Church. Then we will try to see what her life must have been like during these years after Christ's Ascension. Finally, we will consider what we can know about her passage from this life into the life and glory of heaven.

A) MARY AT PENTECOST

In the Acts of the Apostles we are told that Mary was in the upper room on Pentecost, united with all the others in prayer, preparing themselves for the coming of the Holy Spirit. Mary's prayers, united with those of the others, must have been very powerful in moving God to send the Holy Spirit upon the apostles and thus inaugurate his Church that was to last until the end of time. When St. Luke tells us that the Holy Spirit came, in what seemed like fiery tongues, and that these tongues separated and came to rest on the heads of all present, some Fathers of the Church conclude from this that the Holy Spirit came first upon Mary and only then did these fiery tongues separate to come and rest upon the others present.

In this we find symbolized that all the graces coming from the Holy Spirit upon the Church were to come through Mary as being the mother of the Church and the Mediatrix of all graces. As Mary had a vital place in the coming of Jesus at the Incarnation and in the work of our redemption on Calvary, it was only fitting that she should have a vital place in the founding of the Church and in the dispensing of the fruits of salvation down the ages.

Now that Jesus was no longer with them, the apostles must have found how much Mary was like Jesus himself. Hence, they naturally turned to her for advice and encouragement even as before they used to turn to Jesus. However, in helping them Mary's role was as mother and not as Lord and Master. In the Church Mary would compliment Jesus as a mother compliments a father for their children. Therefore, just as the apostles and early Christians found in Jesus a loving Father and Master, so in Mary they found a loving Mother and perfect model for that inner life of the kingdom which they themselves and all the faithful should now live with Jesus. Without Mary something would be wanting in the Church even as something is wanting in any family that has no mother.

B) MARY IN THE EARLY CHURCH

If after Pentecost, Mary is not mentioned in the Gospel it is because the apostles and the evangelists were completely taken up with bringing Jesus' message of salvation to the world. However, Mary's prayerful contribution to the early Church was certainly far more profound than we might at first imagine from the little we hear of her in the canonical books of the New Testament. Once the Christian message was well established in the known world and Mary was in heaven, the attention of the early Church began to turn to Mary and her role in the work of our salvation. It was then that the faithful became interested in Mary and started to celebrate her various feast days.

While Mary's place in the early Church was less spectacular than that of the apostles, it was far more important. Her place consisted in living the inner life of the kingdom which the apostles were engaged in proclaiming to the world. And that inner life is of the very essence of the Christian message, namely, the personal union of every human person, with and through Jesus, in his own divine life of mutual knowledge and love within the Trinity. Living that inner life is the essential goal of the kingdom of God, which Jesus came to establish. Its external ministry is only a means to promote that inner life, a means which will one day come to an end. All Christians, all mankind, therefore are called to live that inner life of friendship with God, which St. Peter describes as a participation in the divine nature. (2 Pet. 1:3-4) It is this inner life Mary lived after Pentecost and she did so with the greatest possible perfection so that she is the perfect model for all the faithful.

Living the interior spiritual life: the very life of God himself, is the end and goal of salvation history. Surprisingly we often find this inner life lived more faithfully by the laity than by the clergy. The reason seems to be, that the laity are generally forced, as it were, to live it by reason of the demands and difficulties of their daily lives. The clergy, on the other hand, are so taken up with the knowledge and work of the ministry, that they are inclined to think that knowing the spiritual life is equal to living it. Hence, those priests who live that inner life most faithfully will be the ones who are most fruitful in the works of their ministry, whereas priests who neglect the living of that inner life, are the ones who are today dissenting from the Magisterium and leading so many of the faithful astray.

Seeing Mary's place in the Church in this way should help us see why there was no need for Mary to be a priest, even though, on Calvary, she was more fully united with Jesus in his supreme sacrifice than any Christian priest will ever be. The priesthood is one of those gifts not given to all. As St. Paul said, "Not all are apostles, teachers, preachers," (and we can add, priests) for if all the members had the same function the whole body would be destroyed. In the Old Testament the priesthood was reserved to a single family, and in the New Testament, according to the Christian tradition of 2,000 years, it has been reserved to men to the exclusion of women.

The priesthood is a ministry of service and not one of power and prestige, which seems to be what so many women are looking for in their desire for the priesthood. St. Paul tells us that we should be desirous of that higher gift, namely, charity and not some passing ministerial function in the Church. This is also what Jesus was implying when he said, "It is not those who are united with him through some human bond or relationship who were his mother, brother and sister, but those who are united with him through charity, by doing the will of his Father in heaven." (cf. Mk. 3:33-35)

C) THE LIFE OF MARY AFTER PENTECOST

After Pentecost, how did Mary live her life? How long did she live before being taken up into heaven? Where did she spend these years? We have no clear answer to these questions. There seems to be a general belief that Mary lived to the age of seventy. If Mary was 15 at the time of the Annunciation and Jesus was 33 at the time of his death, Mary would have been about 48 or 50 at the time of Pentecost. Hence, it is believed that she lived for 20 years after the departure of Jesus from this world.

Since Jesus had committed Mary to the care of St. John, she must have lived these 20 years with him and apparently in or around Jerusalem. That seems to be the conclusion we can gather from the writings of St. Paul. St. Paul was converted about three years after Pentecost. In his epistle to the Galatians he tells us that after his conversion he went off to Arabia for three years and only after that did he visit Jerusalem and stayed with Peter for 15 days. (Gal. 1:18) It was 14 years after this that he went again to Jerusalem with Barnabas and Titus (Gal. 2:1) and this time he says he met James, Peter and John. (Gal. 2:9) This visit must have been about 20 years after Pentecost at which time St. John was still in Jerusalem. If this is all true, and St. Paul swears it is, then Mary must have lived in or around Jerusalem the last 20 years of her life, unless John went elsewhere for a time and Mary went with him, which is not very likely.

Apparently, all the apostles did not start out on missionary journeys right after Pentecost, as we are inclined to think. When the persecution broke out, after the death of St. Stephen, we are told that everyone except the apostles fled to the country districts of Judea and Samaria.(Acts 8:1) No doubt the apostles were able to remain because of Gamaliel's advice that the Jewish leaders should not kill the apostles, but that this affair should be allowed to die of itself should it not be of God. (Acts 5:38) From this we can conclude that St John remained in Jerusalem with Mary, at least until after the departure of Mary from this life.

As to how Mary spent these years, we can be sure it was mainly in contemplation. These must have been the most contemplative years of her life. Now that she knew Jesus was actually God she must have ruminated over all the events of her life with that new vision in mind. She must have become lost in wonder at the ways of God and his condescension in living with herself and among men.

Jesus was always the center of her life, but now she was united with him more deeply through a more enlightened faith and love. Her faith must have been so strong that it was only a step from vision. Her daily union with Jesus in the Eucharist and the Mass must have been the high point of her day. What emotions filled her heart when she reflected on how humble and submissive Jesus was to herself and Joseph, knowing now that he was truly God. Then there were her conversations with John who recalled so many of the sayings of Jesus that referred to his divinity and his oneness with the Father and the Holy Spirit.

During these years, as Mary watched the growth and vicissitudes of the Church; she prayed ardently for the Church and for the salvation of every human person. For she loved them all as her own children, even, as being Jesus himself. We cannot know the effectiveness of prayer, except in a general way, for seldom can we attribute a particular good effect to the prayer of this or that person. However, we can be sure that Mary's prayers were extremely effective towards the growth of the early Church and for the fervor of the early Christians even to the point of martyrdom. During these years Mary's life was truly hidden in God.

D) MARY'S PASSAGE INTO ETERNITY

As the apostles became more separated by reason of their apostolic work, Mary's influence upon them and the early Christians became less necessary, so that her physical presence on earth was no longer needed. Then too, her inner life with Jesus during these years, nourished especially by the daily Eucharist, must have come to a point where her longing to be with Jesus was continual. She had arrived at a stage in her life and union with Jesus when she was living more in heaven than on earth. Her passage, then, from this life into the next, must have been much like the gradual opening of a flower into full bloom.

Since it is very likely that Mary did not experience death, we can suppose that her passage took place through some kind of mystical trance wherein she was thought to be dead and was buried. The legend, based on some apocryphal texts, which states that St. Thomas arrived too late to see Mary before her passage, but wanted to see her for one last time, may possess some traditional truth. When they opened the tomb for him, her body was gone.

Mary's bodily Assumption into heaven is now a dogma of faith which we must believe. It is no longer just a pious belief. How her Assumption took place in the physical order we do not know, but surely it was not beyond God's power to effect.

I like to muse on what that first moment of entering into heaven must have been like for Mary. She must have been overwhelmed with joy and wonder on seeing Jesus in all the beauty and glory of his humanity and his Divinity. What an embrace of love she experienced when the immensity of God's fullness of being, enfolded her in the mutual knowledge and love of the three divine persons. United with Jesus as his spouse, she finds herself to be known and loved in him by the Father and the Holy Spirit; and in union with Jesus she finds herself capable of knowing and loving the Father and the Holy Spirit with Jesus' own knowledge and love. These are things we can state in words, but can never comprehend or experience in this life.

While Mary rejoices in the fullness of her eternal happiness, she is still the mother of all mankind, her children here on earth. Appointed by God to be our Mediatrix, her motherly solicitude is all the more powerful now that she is in heaven and no longer limited by our earthly condition. The very immensity of her own glory makes her all the more anxious to lead all her children, still struggling on earth, into the arms of her Jesus, that they may come to know the same happiness and Joy that is hers. Mary is still our mother now, but in heaven she will be our Queen uniting us with Jesus our King, who will take us up with Mary into the eternal embrace of the Trinity.

PART III

HOW MARY IS GOD'S
SUPREME MASTERPIECE

MARY: GOD'S SUPREME MASTERPIECE

INTRODUCTION

In the first part of this book I have shown by principles of reason and faith, the unique place Mary has been given in God's great work of creation and salvation. In the second part I have shown how Mary, in her earthly life, freely and perfectly corresponded with God in his plan for mankind, so that she is our perfect model in living the Christian life and also our bond of unity with Christ in human friendship. Here in part three, I want to show how Mary is God's Supreme Masterpiece: that in his present order of creation, he could not have made a mere creature to be more perfect than Mary.

Mary's definition of her Self: When Bernadette at Lourdes asked Mary who she was, Mary replied, "I am the Immaculate Conception." In these words Mary has given us a definition of herself. A definition should distinguish the one defined from all other things, so that it stands out as unique in itself without any danger of being confused with something else.

When Mary called herself "A Conception," she gave, what philosophers call, the genus of the definition: that general class of reality to which she belongs. Here the term "Conception" is used to mean a "creature" that is, one who exists only because it is a concept in the mind of the creator to which concept he has willed to give an existence apart from himself.

When Mary says she is "The Immaculate" conception, she is giving us the differentiation: that particular attribute of being immaculate or absolutely perfect, that distinguishes her from all other individuals in the genus of creature. Mary then is "The Immaculate Conception:" that immaculate creature conceived in the mind of God that is absolutely perfect, possessing everything God can possibly give to a mere creature. Also, as a free creature, Mary is one who has freely conformed her will to God's will without the slightest deviation or sin throughout her whole life.

In what perfection consists: It is a general principle in theology that the greatness or perfection of a creature consists in its conformity to, and unity with God who is the archetype of all perfections. Since we cannot conceive of a creature being more united with God than through a unity of person, Jesus, by reason of the hypostatic union, is as man the most perfect fruit of God's creative power. However Christ, being a divine person, in not a mere creature in the full sense of that word. Therefore, we can claim for Mary the prerogative of being the most perfect *mere creature* God could create in the present order of creation, if not in every possible order of creations. Indeed, we cannot imagine a creature more intimately united with God in his Trinitarian life than Mary. She is the Daughter of the Father, Mother of the Son and Spouse of the Holy Spirit.

Division of subject matter: In this third part I will first show that all God's works have to be absolutely perfect according to the end he has in view. Secondly, that God has achieved that absolute perfection of his creation in Jesus and Mary. And thirdly, that all mankind is given to share in the absolute perfection of Jesus and Mary according to their degree of union with them in charity. In the fourth and last chapter, I will consider the final and perfect fulfillment of God's whole plan of creation and salvation as it will be in heaven, so far as we can know it in this present life.

CHAPTER I

ALL GOD'S WORKS MUST BE ABSOLUTELY PERFECT

A) WHY GOD'S WORKS MUST HE PERFECT

Since God is infinite in wisdom, power and goodness he cannot do any work that is not absolutely perfect according to the final goal or plan he has in view. If a better way existed, God would have to choose that better way, otherwise there would be an imperfection in God, which is impossible. Hence, difficult as that may be for us to understand, the means God chooses to employ in order to achieve any goal must be the very best. This applies even to the use he makes of evil. If God could achieve his goal as perfectly or more perfectly without allowing evil, he would have to choose that better means.

Man, then, by his free will, can never frustrate God's definitive plan; he can only frustrate his own sharing in that plan. That God can achieve his goal more perfectly by allowing evil in his creation than by eliminating it, is a manifestation of God's infinite wisdom and supreme dominion over his creation that we will never fully grasp, but which we must be willing to accept on faith.

God's final goal is something spiritual: We will better understand God's ways of acting if we remember that God's plan is something spiritual and not something material. The material creation is only a means God uses for a spiritual end. As we have seen, the only spiritual realities that exist are knowledge and love. But these are found only in intellectual beings or persons who have the capacity and the desire to possess all truth and goodness. To give to man the fullness of all truth and goodness is God's supreme goal. Everything else is but a means to that end. At present we have only some truth and goodness, but we desire the fullness of all truth and goodness in a union of mutual knowledge and love with someone who is all truth and goodness, namely, God.

In human friendship, especially in marriage, man can find some fulfillment of his longing for truth and goodness, but it is never fully adequate since all human beings are limited and can never give us that fullness of truth and goodness we desire. Then too, human friendship is easily hindered by selfishness and other obstacles, so that even the limited happiness of marriage is often absent.

Therefore, the perfect happiness and fulfillment which we long for can only be found in a loving union with God who is all truth and goodness. And God will never fail us although we can, and often do, fail him through the abuse of our freedom.

Our part in God's plan: In itself we can not frustrate God's plan. However, since his plan requires our free acceptance, we can frustrate our share in it. That is where we often fail. We want to be our own bosses and follow our own desires, ideas, and goals. We are self-asserting children.

Parents are responsible for the existence of their children, but how their children will use that existence is not wholly under the parent's control. Certainly parents must do all they can to help their children develop and use all their capabilities, but still the children can thwart their parents loving plans if they will not cooperate sufficiently. So it is with God's plan for us; we are free to do our part or not, but then it is we who will suffer, not God's plan. Even our freedom is a means in God's hands. He can and does use our failures to further his plan.

B) IN WHAT GOD'S PRESENT PLAN CONSISTS

Let us see in what God's present plan for creation consists. God's purpose in creating is to give us the highest possible share in his own divine life and happiness. He wants to make us gods insofar as that is possible for him to effect and for our capacity to receive. Since he cannot make us gods by nature, he has willed to make us gods by participation.

Being gods by participation: Let us see what that means. Our body is not intellectual and yet it participates in our intellectual life in a most intimate way. It is through our body that we speak, hear, write and make things. We cannot imagine how our body could share more in our intellectual life without itself becoming intellectual. In much the same way God wants to give us to participate in his divine life, even to the point that cannot share more in his divine life without ourselves becoming divine.

The comparison of our body sharing in our intellectual life is not fully adequate in conveying what our sharing in Cod's divine life will be like, for our body is not a person. Try to imagine how much closer would be our union were our body a person. There would be the added intimacy of love and friendship greater than that found between husband and wife, child and parents. What such a participation in God's divine life would be like is difficult for us to imagine. It would be somewhat like the intimacy between Jesus and his humanity.

Jesus' humanity was not divine yet it participated in his divine life by working miracles, uttering prophecies and now shares in his glory and divine Sonship in heaven. Here too, Christ's humanity is not a person, but, if it were, what a loving union would exist between them. In a sense, however, we are the person of Christ's humanity. As members of his Church, his Mystical Body, we are Christ's bride. Hence, in taking on our human nature Jesus has taken all of us into himself. We are the person of his humanity, so to say, and as such we share in a loving friendship with him in his divinity. We have a mystical oneness with Jesus' humanity that we must acknowledge without fully understanding.

C) HOW GOD MAKES HIS PRESENT CREATION PERFECT

God's divine life, in which we are called to participate, is one of friendship: the mutual knowledge and love that exists between the three divine persons in the Trinity. This God wants to share with us, but for that he needs our free acceptance. Since he cannot force our free acceptance, he is limited to manifesting his love in such a way as to most effectively win our acceptance.

A twofold plan: From divine revelation we know that God has willed to call us to such an acceptance through a twofold plan: one conditional and the other definitive. He allowed his first conditional plan to fail so that he might manifest his mercy and goodness in the highest possible way through a second definitive plan. At the same time he used this approach to make us experience our helplessness and misery in such a way that we should be compelled, as it were, to see our dire need of him and his friendship.

God also wants to move us to accept his offer of friendship in the most total and perfect way possible. He knows that our share in his happiness will be determined by the measure of our acceptance. Hence, he is much like a mother who seeks to move her child to attain the highest possible honors in his studies and the highest possible accomplishments in his adult life. God wants to move us to attain the summit of holiness; he wants us to be perfect even as he is perfect.

God so desires this because, in his love for us, he wants us to be as happy as he is himself and he knows that we can find that happiness only in a loving friendship with himself. As St. Therese of Lisieux observed, God's love for us is so great and so pent up within him, that his heart is at a breaking point, because so few are willing to accept his love in all its fullness.

How God's plan is most perfect in itself: In spite of our failures to respond fully to his love, God has managed to bring his plan for creation to its highest possible fulfillment and perfection in Jesus and Mary.

All God's works should be stamped with his trademark of absolute perfection. This we certainly find in Jesus' active redemption, for we cannot imagine how God could give us more than he has actually done so by redeeming us and uniting us with himself in and through Jesus. But passive redemption: that is, the perfect reception of all that Jesus has won for us, where do we find that in all its fullness? Surely God wants us to receive as much as he can give and, since he cannot be thwarted in his plan, he must have established some means whereby that is possible. This he has done in Mary. Only in Mary do we find that perfect fruit of redemption received in all its fullness. All other men and women, even the greatest saints have been tarnished by sin and are like broken vessels that have been repaired.

But surely Mary cannot be the only perfect fruit of God's greatest work. St. Paul, when speaking of the Church says, "Christ made her (the Church) clean by washing her in water and a form of words so that when he took her to himself she would be glorious and without spot or wrinkle or anything like that but wholly spotless." (Eph. 5:27) If these words, which can only be true of Mary, are applied to the whole Church, then somehow all Christ's members must be able to share in Mary's perfect passive redemption. And why not? If Jesus can share with us his perfect active redemption, why can he not give Mary to share with us her perfect passive redemption?

God can give us to share not only in what he gives directly to us but also through what he gives to others. Do not children share in the gifts of their parents, and a wife in those of her husband and he in hers. There is no reason then why Jesus, who can give us to share in the fullness of his active redemption through our faith and love in him, cannot also give us to share in the fullness of Mary's passive redemption through faith and love in what Jesus has made Mary to be to us. Thus in Jesus and Mary God's great work of creation and redemption has reached a perfection wholly worthy of God's infinite wisdom, power and goodness.

D) HOW EACH INDIVIDUAL SHARES IN THE PERFECTION OF GOD'S PLAN

What God has so perfectly achieved in Jesus and Mary is now the permanent endowment of our human race in such a way that it can never be lost. However, each individual is free to share or enter into that endowment according to his own free choice, that is, according to the degree of his charity, whereby he unites himself with Jesus and Mary in loving friendship.

We can see something of how this is to be achieved in the example of a loving family. The father and mother have, in a mature way, everything that pertains to the perfection of adult human life. And they want to share this with their children in the most perfect way. However, they can only do so to the extent that their children love and trust them and come to them to receive from their fullness. If one of their children should choose to run away from home, he would then have no part in what they could give him. Those who choose to remain under the loving care of their parents will enjoy everything their parents can give them but only according to their confidence in their parents and their cooperation with the wise designs of their parents. In this way, in time, they can become as perfect as their parents in a mature adult life.

It is much the same in our relationship with Jesus and Mary. They love us as their children and are more than anxious to share everything they have with us in all its fullness. When we give ourselves to them in child-like love and confidence they share with us the fullness of God's spiritual gifts. All that they have becomes ours to the degree of our union with them in loving friendship.

In heaven all will possess the fullness of God's perfect work of creation as found in Jesus and Mary, but according to the capacity of each one, determined by their charity. Thus it is that the saints, while possessing the fullness of eternal life, will still differ in glory like the stars in brightness according to their different degrees of charity.

Jesus has actually won back for us all that we lost in Adam in a higher and more perfect way. Therefore, when we become one with Jesus in baptism we receive everything we lost and more, but not all at the same time. The spiritual gifts, these we receive back immediately: forgiveness of all sin and punishment and the life of sanctifying grace whereby we become partakers of the divine nature. But the preternatural gifts: freedom from death and suffering and from the rebellion of the passions, these we will receive back only at the moment of our death. God has willed it so since that is more profitable for our spiritual growth: keeping us humble and dependent upon God.

CHAPTER II

HOW JESUS AND MARY ARE GOD'S MASTERPIECES

Since we are called to share in the absolute perfection and holiness of Jesus and Mary, let us consider in what their perfection consists so as to better understand the gift God is giving us in them.

The perfection of the creature is found in its degree of oneness or conformity with God who is the exemplar of all perfection and being. As should be evident, no one is more perfectly united with God and conformed to him than Jesus and Mary: Jesus by reason of his union with God as a divine person, and Mary by reason of her perfect union with Jesus in human friendship. Hence, no one can unite us more perfectly with God in divine friendship than Jesus, the God-man, and no one can unite us more perfectly with Jesus in human friendship than Mary his perfect spouse. As Jesus is our perfect mediator with God in divine friendship so Mary is our perfect Mediatrix with Jesus in human friendship. Jesus is God's supreme masterpiece of creation in an absolute sense, but Mary is God's supreme masterpiece of creation in the limited sense of a mere creature.

In Scripture their unique roles are indicated when it is said of both of them that they are full of grace, that is, full of all that God can give them according to their place in the work of redemption.

Thus, St. John in his Gospel, tells us that Jesus, "Was full of grace and truth." (Jn. 1: 14) and St. Luke has the angel saluting Mary with the words, "Hail full of grace." (Lk. 1:28) Jesus has the fullness of grace by reason of his active redemption and Mary by reason of her passive redemption.

In this chapter I would like to consider that total perfection of Jesus and Mary in which we are called to share by a union of loving friendship with them.

A) THE ABSOLUTE PERFECTION
OF JESUS IN HIS HUMANITY

Christ in his humanity is certainly the most perfect work of God's creation. Jesus as man is so united to a divine person that we must say of this man, "He is God." This is something we would never have thought possible. It involves a number of things.

Jesus is perfect man and perfect God: Jesus has two complete natures: the divine nature and the human nature. When we first try to picture the Incarnation to ourselves, we are inclined to imagine Christ's body as being his human nature and his soul as being his divine nature. Of course that is wholly wrong; Jesus' human nature was complete with body and soul and his divine nature was also complete.

The mystery of the Incarnation lies in the fact that the second person of the Trinity is the *person* living and acting in both natures without any mixing of the natures themselves. Since the person acting in Christ's human nature was divine, all his actions as man have the value of his divine person.

Now it is impossible for us to imagine a creature being elevated to a higher dignity and union with God than the humanity of Jesus. But what is more, Jesus, being God, lived the human life of a creature in its proper relationship with God to the utmost perfection. In other words, Jesus, in his humanity, acknowledged God's supreme rights over him and lived in humility, obedience and love before God as behooves a creature before its creator. He lived our human life with the utmost perfection and holiness and that means in a union of loving friendship with God, perfect in knowledge and love.

Jesus was perfect in knowledge: Christ's union with his Father in mutual knowledge was absolutely perfect. There was nothing the Father knew that Jesus did not know. As Jesus said, "Everything the Father has is mine." (Jn. 16:15) It could not be otherwise seeing that Jesus could say to Philip "Do you not believe that I am in the Father and the Father is in me?" (Jn. 14:10) Their knowledge was equally shared: "The Son can do nothing by himself: he can only do what he sees the Father doing, and whatever the Father does the Son does too." (Jn. 5:19) indeed, Jesus knows the Father even as he is known by the Father, and so he could say. "No one knows the Son but the Father and no one knows the Father but the Son and those to whom the Son reveals him. "(Lk. 10:22)

Jesus was perfect in love: Jesus was perfectly united with his Father in mutual love. He was certainly conscious of his Father's love for himself as seen in his words, "The Father loves his Son and shows him everything he does himself." (Jn. 5:20) And in the Father's words, "This is my beloved Son in whom I am well pleased." (Mt. 3:17)

That Jesus loved his Father in return is seen in the words, "I always do the things that please him." (Jn. 8:29) And, "My food is to do the will of the one who sent me." (Jn. 4:34) To do his Father's will was the very reason of his coming, "I have come from heaven, not to do my own will but to do the will of the one who sent me." (Jn. 6:38)

The essential duty of a creature is to do what he was made to do. As someone has expressed it. "What evil this that craft should fail its master's will in all fulfill." Therefore just as it is our duty to love God by keeping his commandments, so the man, Jesus, loved his Father by keeping his Father's commandments. Hence, his words, "If you keep my commandments you will remain in my love, even as I have kept my Father's commandments and remain in his love." (Jn. 15:10)

Jesus' human love for his Father reached its highest peak on Calvary. In that supreme act he sacrificed himself as man in perfect submission to his Father's will in order to make amends for our sins and to restore us to friendship with his Father. On Calvary Jesus fulfilled the two great commandments of the law, in the most perfect way. In that supreme act he immolated his humanity in loving submission to his Father's will. In that same act he loved us, his fellow men and women in the most perfect way by laying down his life for love of us. In so doing he freed us from the debt of our sins and gave us a share in his own eternal happiness. No creature could possibly be more united with God in mutual knowledge and love than Jesus in his humanity, and therefore, we ourselves, who are as the person of that humanity, his bride.

What Jesus did as man is for us: All that Jesus did as man he did for us, his bride, his other self. Jesus as God did not need to be saved, but Jesus as man, as being ourselves, needed to be saved. Therefore, it is we who are saved in the sacrifice of his humanity. If Jesus sanctified himself as man, it was that we might be sanctified in him. (cf. Jn. 17:19) St Athanasius asserts as a principle, "Whatever is written of Jesus in a human way should be referred to the common human race of men. Therefore, when it is said that Jesus was exalted to the right hand of God this applies to us, for as God, Jesus is always exalted at God's right hand."

From this we see that all that Jesus acquired and merited in his humanity he acquired and merited for us. And that is why St. John could write, "He who has the Son has life, he who does not have the Son does not have life." (1 Jn. 5:12) It is only in Jesus, in his humanity, that we are united with God in his divine life. Jesus in his humanity is our bridegroom but in that same humanity we are his bride, his other self as man. Husband and wife in marriage become one body, so Jesus and we ourselves through grace, through love, become one regenerated mankind. As Jesus' humanity is perfectly united with his divinity so we, as the fullness of his humanity, are perfectly united with God in Jesus.

B) THE ABSOLUTE PERFECTION
OF MARY AS A CREATURE

As Jesus unites us with his Father in perfect divine friendship so Mary unites us with Jesus in perfect human friendship. Jesus, in his humanity unites us with his Father in divine friendship only to the extent that we are one with him as man. But no one was more perfectly united with Jesus as man than Mary. Hence, only in her can we ourselves be perfectly united with Jesus in human friendship.

Here I would like to consider first how Mary completes Jesus in his social nature as man and then how she is absolutely perfect in every way in her human friendship with Jesus.

Mary completes Jesus in his social nature as man: Jesus in his social nature as man was incomplete without his other self, even as every man and woman needs a relationship of mutual knowledge and love with another equal person. In fact we need such a relationship with every human individual for only in this way can we possess ourselves in the fullness of our humanity. Every human being possesses something of humanity that is unique and which no one else has in the same way. Thus we cannot have the fullness of humanity without being united with what is unique in all other human beings. Because of our human limitations in this life such a union with every other individual is impossible. Hence, the number of our friendships at present are limited to relatives and a number of friends. And if such a friendship is to include the body, as in marriage, then it is even limited to one of the opposite sex. However, in the next life, we will indeed have such a union with every other individual as part of our total happiness.

Jesus in his humanity had these same needs and limitations. Hence, during his mortal life, his friendships with others were limited in number. And his human friendship was fully perfect only with one person, namely, Mary who, as his mystical bride was the new Eve united with Jesus the new Adam. Being one with Jesus as his bride, Mary was also one with him as the head and leader of a new human race, that of redeemed mankind. Therefore, while Jesus is as the king of this new human race, Mary is as our Queen, his bride, who lived with him his most perfect life of human friendship with his Father. This she did especially when sharing in his supreme sacrifice on Calvary.

As we have seen, we ourselves, the Church, all mankind, are as the person of Christ's humanity: that sinful bride Jesus has taken to himself. But during his mortal life it was Mary who lived with him as such, by consenting to and accepting his saving sacrifice on Calvary in the name of all mankind. She did this with the utmost perfection possible to a mere creature. Mary not only received from God every possible gift and grace he could give a mere creature, and that with the utmost perfection, she did the same in freely using and cooperating with all his gifts.

Mary has every possible gift and grace: Through the foreseen merits of Jesus, Mary was gifted by God beyond all other creatures. From the first moment of her creation Mary received her human nature in all its pristine and original beauty, just as it came forth from the creative hands of God in our first parents. By God's free gift of grace she was created spotless, untarnished by original sin. Hence, she was not subject to any of the effects of original sin save that of suffering, which Jesus himself willed to accept as the most powerful means to reveal and exercise love. All her faculties were harmonized under the control of her will so that she did not experience concupiscence or that conflict arising from the desires of the senses against the higher aspirations of her mind and will. Everything in her nature moved her to aspire to know the truth and to love the good, that is, God.

Mary was also enriched with the fullness of supernatural graces. From the first moment of her existence she was united with God in loving friendship through sanctifying grace. She was also given a number of unique privileges besides that of her Immaculate Conception, and these united her with God in the closest possible way. She was given to be the mother of the Messiah, the Son of God our Lord Jesus Christ, and also to be his bride and spouse in his work of salvation. As his spouse she acted in our place offering our consent and acceptance to Jesus in his work of our salvation. Hence, she can be truly called our co-redeemer with Jesus. By reason of all these privileges she was united with God, in Jesus, in a way beyond all other creatures.

Mary's perfect correspondence with God's grace: Mary's personal and free correspondence with all the gifts and graces God had given her was also most perfect. By her first conscious and free act of will, Mary accepted God as her creator and his offer of divine friendship, given in sanctifying grace, in the most total and perfect way. And in that first act of acceptance she persevered and grew throughout her whole life through a deep perception of her total dependence on God. This kept her in a very profound humility before God. Throughout her entire life she never committed the least sin or imperfection, so that her will was never out of conformity with God's will in the slightest degree. It is difficult for us to conceive how a frail human creature could be so perfect in her knowledge and love of God, and in such control of all her faculties as never to sin in the slightest way. The only possible explanation is that she was completely possessed by the Holy Spirit and guided by his inspirations in everything she did, and that she was always perfectly docile and generous in following his every inspiration and guidance.

Mary was perfectly united with God through Faith, Hope and Love: God's greatest gift to mankind is our call to share his own divine life of friendship: to be united with God, as he is in himself, in all the riches of his ineffable being, and not merely as he can be known through his creation. But in this life we can only know God, as he is in himself, through **Faith**, that is, through believing what he has told us about himself, especially through Jesus Christ. And we can unite ourselves with him as such, only through **Hope** and **Love** based on that **Faith**. Hence, in this life, our friendship with God can only be lived through the three theological virtues of Faith, Hope and Love. While Love is the greatest of these virtues, Faith is the most fundamental for we can only hope in and love someone according to our knowledge of him. Although we cannot know the inner life of Mary and how she lived these theological virtues, still we can see something of it in the way she responded to the various events of her life as found in the Gospel.

Mary was perfect in Faith: In the Gospel we find Mary's faith as something exceptional. The first witness we have to its greatness is found in those words of Elizabeth, "Blessed is she who believed that the promises made her by the Lord would be fulfilled." (Lk. 1:45) Mary believed that she would become the mother of the Messiah through God's divine power without the loss of her virginity. She also believed that her child was the promised Messiah and in that belief she never faltered throughout her whole life.

We see her faith again in her ready acceptance of the many events of divine providence in her life which she did not clearly understand at the time, such as the decree of Caesar that required her trip to Bethlehem, the flight into Egypt, and the three day loss. Her faith in Jesus was manifest at Cana where she did not doubt that Jesus would solve the problem she brought to his attention, even though at first he seemed to refuse her request. Certainly her faith proved itself beyond compare on Calvary where she witnessed the apparent utter defeat of Jesus, yet she never doubted his final victory. When all the apostles had lost faith, Mary's faith remained firm and unshaken.

Mary was perfect in Hope: As Mary's faith was perfect so too her hope. She never doubted that God would fulfill all that he had promised concerning her son Jesus. She had many occasions to trust in God's providential care in the unforeseeable future, like the flight into Egypt. She had to hope against hope during Christ's public ministry when the opposition against Jesus began to grow, and finally destroyed him. Even in the face of Calvary her hope never wavered. She was certain that Jesus would triumph in the end even if she may not have known that it would be through his resurrection from death. After Calvary, of all the followers of Jesus, Mary alone retained hope in Christ's final victory. And her hope was richly rewarded on Easter morning. That same hope sustained her during those many years she had to remain on earth after the Ascension of Jesus into heaven.

Mary was perfect in Love: As Mary's faith and hope were unparalleled, so too her love, her charity, both for God and for her fellow men and women. That she consecrated her virginity to God at an early age reveals her deep understanding and love of God as her supreme good to be loved above all else. Her ardent prayers for the coming of the Messiah and her acceptance of the responsibility of being his mother with all the sufferings she must have foreseen, could only spring from her great love for God and for the good of all mankind. But it was on Calvary that her love reached its supreme peak. There she offered in sacrifice to God what was more precious to her than her own life: her son Jesus whom she loved more than herself.

Abraham was willing to offer his son to God in sacrifice; Mary actually did so: a son far more loved, and by an infinitely more painful sacrifice. If Abraham was blessed by God because of his willingness to sacrifice his son, with the promise that in his seed all the nations of the world would be blessed, what must be the blessings Mary has received for the sacrifice of her Divine Son?

How can we doubt that God has made her the mother and queen of all mankind and the Mediatrix of all the graces Jesus has won for the human race? Like the heart of Jesus, Mary's heart is an abyss of love which the human mind will never fully plumb in this life. No wonder she is seen in Scripture as unique and perfect, as one who has surpassed all others.

CHAPTER III

ALL MANKIND IS CALLED TO SHARE IN THE PERFECTION OF JESUS AND MARY

In Jesus and Mary God's work of creation has reached an absolute perfection most worthy of God. Jesus in his humanity was perfectly united with God. No created nature could be more perfectly one with God than through a unity of persons. The person of that created nature is God himself. Also Mary, as a mere creature, is so united with Jesus and through Jesus with God, that here too, we cannot imagine how a mere creature could be taken up into God's divine life in a more perfect way. In Jesus and Mary, God's work of creation has achieved an absolute perfection wholly worthy of God.

We are **now** being offered a share, a participation in their absolute perfection and union with God. Nothing we can do can detract from God's perfect work as present in Jesus and Mary. We can only determine the extent to which we ourselves choose to accept and share in their perfection. If one chooses to have nothing at all to do with it, then, he is left with nothing but himself and that is hell: an intellectual creature separated from all truth and goodness and therefore a person totally unfulfilled and frustrated. Those who do choose to be a part of God's gift will share in the perfection of Jesus and Mary according to the degree of their charity. In this chapter I would like to consider the nature of our sharing in the perfection of Jesus and Mary: what it is that Jesus and Mary have to share with us and how we should live our lives so as to share fully in all their riches. Then I will explain what it is that determines the degree of our sharing in their riches.

A) THE NATURE OF OUR SHARING IN THE PERFECTION OF JESUS AND MARY

To understand the nature of our sharing in the perfection of Jesus and Mary we will need to use some comparisons like the social unity of the family and the organic unity of the vine and branch. However, to be helped by these comparisons and not hindered by their limitations we must keep in mind certain points that are special to the nature of our sharing in God's divine life. These special points I would like to consider first.

1. Preliminary information:
Our union with God is something spiritual: While we must use sensible comparisons to help us understand the nature of our union with God in his divine life we must remember that this unity is something spiritual. Therefore it consists in knowledge and love. But knowledge and love only exist in intellectual beings or persons. Hence, we can share in the absolute perfection of Jesus and Mary only by a life of mutual knowledge and love.

We see something of this in marriage. In human love, husband and wife find such joy in their mutual knowledge and love of each other, that, if they had no material needs; they would feel that nothing was wanting to their perfect happiness. We see it also in the life of prayer. When one is experiencing the presence and love of God in prayer he finds such happiness therein that he would not exchange it for any material. satisfaction. We should not be surprised then, that our union with God through Jesus and Mary must consist in the mutual knowledge and love of friendship.

Our union with God is something real: Although this union is something spiritual, it is all the same **real** in the highest sense. We will be so united with Jesus that St. Paul can write, "You who have been baptized into Christ have put on the person of Christ." (Gal. 3:27) We will share in all Christ has as though we were Christ himself. So real is this union that all Christ's merits and holiness will be ours as well as his. That is why Jesus could say, "For their sake I sanctify myself that they may be sanctified in truth." (Jn. 17:19) We are so taken up with Jesus in his divine life with his Father that just as Jesus could say to his Father, "All I have is yours and all you have is Mine," (Jn. 17:10) so Jesus can say to us, as to the elder son of the prodigal son, "My son you are always with me and all I have is yours." (Lk. 15:31) All the Father has Jesus has and all Jesus has we have in him. Our union is real and therefore our sharing is real, so real that it is like the sharing that exists between the three divine persons in the Trinity. For this Jesus prayed, "Father may they be one. Father may they be one in us, as you are in me and I am in you." (Jn. 17:21)

Our need of comparisons: Since our sharing in God's divine life is something spiritual, known only through faith, we can only form some concept of its nature using certain familiar comparisons. Of these there are two kinds we can use: those that express a social unity, like the family, and those that express an organic unity, like the vine with its branches. Since our unity with God in his divine life is something personal between persons, we need to use social comparisons to understand the personal aspects of that unity. But since it is also organic we need to use organic comparisons to understand its living bond whereby we are made into one living reality. We also need to unite the two in our mind so as to see our personal relationship with God as a living unity.

Since we are called to a twofold friendship with Jesus, as man and as God, let us first consider the nature of our friendship with Jesus as man by means of social and organic comparisons.

2. The nature of our unity with Jesus as man:
a. By social comparisons: In considering the nature of our unity with Jesus as man there are two social comparisons we can use: that of the family and that of the civil state.

That of the family: In the comparison of the family, Jesus and Mary become as our father and mother and we as their children. Since Mary, by living with Jesus as his new Eve, in our place, had a part in giving us birth with Jesus into the life of grace, we are as their children. Being their children, they want us to grow in our new life until we become as spiritual adults and eventually even as spouses of Jesus in likeness to Mary. Being our parents in this new divine life, Jesus and Mary love us as their own children. They see us as the concrete expression of their mutual love for one another. Indeed, children are a kind of mutual gift of husband and wife to one another. By making his wife pregnant the husband gives her the gift of a child, and the wife by giving birth and raising the child, gives the child back to its father as her gift of love to him. Mary then loves us as Jesus' gift to her and Jesus loves us as Mary's gift to himself. Thus we, their children, are caught up in their own mutual love for one another.

Because parents love their children as themselves, there is nothing they will not share with their children as the need arises. Indeed, everything they ever desired for themselves they want their child to obtain and, if that were possible, even more. The child on its part has only to receive everything from its parents with loving trust and abandonment in order to experience that happy freedom so characteristic of a child's life.

Loving parents find a deep joy in caring for their children, and the children find great security and happiness in being cared for by their parents. We may even ask, who is more happy, the parents in caring for their children or the children in being cared for by their parents? They fulfill one anothers needs and desires to the mutual joy of both. However, should the child refuse its parents love and insist on following its own immature judgment and desires or especially if he should run away from home, he would inflict great pain on his parents and make his own life most miserable.

What parents are to their children in their earthly life, Jesus and Mary are to us in our spiritual life. How good and wise God has been in giving us Jesus and Mary to be as our father and mother in our spiritual life. He has thus provided perfectly for our spiritual needs no less than for our earthly needs. A child needs both the strong guidance of its father and the tender love of its mother.

A child in its relationship with its parents is always free to go directly to its father, at any time, and the father is always pleased when his child does so. However, the father is even more pleased when his child comes to him through his mother, for then, the father experiences the love of both his wife and his child at the same time. So it is that Jesus is more pleased when we come to him through Mary, and Mary is delighted to bring us to Jesus so as to tell him of our good deeds, to make excuse for our faults and to plead for anything we might need. Indeed, and here our comparison falls short, Mary wants us to become like herself, the perfect spouse and bride of Jesus. She wants us to find everything in Jesus as our supreme good and joy even as she does herself. Thus it is that we are called to become united with Jesus in perfect human friendship as his spouse in the likeness of Mary and through Mary.

That of the civil state: We can also consider our union with Jesus and Mary in the likeness of a monarchical state. Then Jesus becomes as our king and Mary as our queen and we as their children and subjects. In the civil state the subjects find a more ample fulfillment of their human needs through the mutual sharing of gifts and talents with a larger group of people. This is done under the guidance of a ruler who gives order and direction to the whole group for the greater good of all.

In such a state the head or ruler can act in the name of all, so that they all become involved in the consequences of his decisions. Thus it was that we were involved in the sin of our first parents, Adam and Eve, who, as the patriarchal heads of our human race, rejected God's offer of divine friendship. But when Jesus and Mary, acting as the new head and ruler of a new regenerated mankind made reparation for that-former sin, they won back for us all we lost in Adam and Eve, but in a higher and more perfect society: a new mankind. Now we, as their children and subjects in that new mankind, share in all the spiritual prosperity they have won for our new mankind.

In Jesus and Mary therefore, we have not only the perfect happiness of family life but also all the blessing of being a part of a great and mighty kingdom of God with all the angels and saints as fellow citizens. In all their gifts we share as children of the same family and state. But we have all these in a spiritual way of which our comparisons can only give us a tiny glimpse.

b. By organic comparisons: Social comparisons help us to see the wonderful person-to-person relationship we have with Jesus in human friendship, but not the closeness of that relationship. That is where organic comparisons can help. That our unity with Jesus is something organic is evident in Scripture. Jesus compares our unity with himself to the vine with its branches, and St. Paul, to the unity of the human body with its head and members. As there is but one life in the vine which flows into all its branches, so there is but one life flowing from Jesus into us. That life is sanctifying grace whereby we share in God's own divine life.

Since the branches of the vine cannot produce a fruit of lesser value than the vine itself, so all our actions done according to the will of Jesus are the actions of Jesus and possess the value and dignity of Jesus himself. The same is true of the comparison of the human body with all its member. Whatever my hand does at my direction is done by me and has the value and importance of my personal dignity. So too, in our union with Jesus, all our actions, performed in conformity with the will of Jesus, are the acts of Jesus and share his infinite value and dignity.

Of course, this is only true when we are in the state of grace and our actions are in conformity with the will of Jesus, with the will of God. If we are not in the state of grace, we are as dead members and eventually we will be cut off from the body should we still be in that state at the moment of death. If we are in the state of grace, but our actions are contrary to God's will, although not in a grave matter, we are then like a paralyzed member that does not respond to the will of Jesus. Hence, they are not the actions of Jesus and have no spiritual value. Here we see the importance and the value of always being in the state of grace and of always doing the will of God. By so doing our whole life has a divine value beyond anything we can imagine.

These social and organic comparisons give us some insight into the nature of our loving friendship with Jesus as man, and into the blessings that union contains for us. But they can never give us to see the full reality of the spiritual and supernatural blessings we have through our union with Jesus, for of such blessings all earthly comparisons are but a mere shadow.

3. The nature of our unity with Jesus as God: Let us now consider the nature of our union of friendship with Jesus as God. Here Jesus is like the son of a king who, by marrying a girl, takes her up with himself into the life of the royal family.

Just as that girl could never become a member of the royal family in any other way, so neither can we become a member of the household of God except through a union of friendship with Jesus comparable to marriage. Jesus alone, by reason of his humanity and divinity, can unite us with God and that is why he is our only mediator with God.

a. By social comparisons: The comparison we will find most helpful here is that of marriage. When considering our friendship with Jesus as man I used the comparison of the family, and how, as the children of Jesus and Mary, our goal is to become spiritual adults so that we ourselves might become the spouses of Jesus in likeness of Mary.

Here, to understand the nature of our union with Jesus as God, we must see ourselves in the likeness of a bride married to the son of a king. In the spousal love of marriage, husband and wife seek their happiness and fulfillment in one another. Indeed, in their deep love for one another they seem to find everything they desire. They find in one another that most basic need of their intellectual nature: to know and to be known, to love and to be loved. And, since the love that unites them should be that of benevolence, they seek the well-being and happiness of the other more than their own; they find more happiness in the other's good than in their own. What they really find is a certain completion of themselves in the other which their social nature requires.

In their mutual relationship the husband is as the leader and the authority with greater strength and drive, while the wife is as the one who receives and follows, offering her husband her loving esteem and confidence. How secure a wife feels while resting in the loving strength and firm support of her husband and how strong and self-reliant he feels when experiencing the tender esteem and loving confidence of his wife. There are psychological differences between man and woman whereby they so complete one another that in a perfect marriage husband and wife would never dream of changing roles.

Between the creature and God, however, there are far greater differences than the psychological differences between man and woman. Because of that the soul of man is always feminine before God. From this we can see how destructive is modern feminism which wants to obliterate the difference between man and woman, and even between God and man, by wanting to make God feminine. God indeed embraces in himself all masculine and feminine perfections but to us, as creatures, he cannot be other than as masculine. To try and make God feminine to us borders on being a contradiction.

Beautiful and wonderful as marriage may be, it is not the final goal and happiness of man. This is very evident when one partner in marriage dies. The one left behind will generally feel so devastated that he or she will think there is nothing left in life to live for. Hence, married people must realize that they need a still higher goal. On the human level they may try to find that higher goal in the perpetuation of themselves in their children. But that will never give them the complete personal fulfillment they desire. By reason of their intellectual nature they want to be united in loving friendship with someone who is all truth and goodness. Hence, they can find their true higher goal only in a loving friendship with God who is all truth and goodness. Of this higher goal, marriage is only a limited image. And yet, if a good marriage can be so wonderful, what must that union be like which is had with him who is all truth and goodness, namely, God? Hence, unless husband and wife in their mutual love strive to help each other come to a higher union of friendship with God, they will never find unending happiness. It can never be truly said of them, "They lived happily ever after."

So it is that we, in becoming united with Jesus **as man** in human friendship as his spouse must, at the same time, live with him **as God** his higher life of friendship with his Father. With Jesus we must love the Father more than ourselves by always accepting and doing the Father's will. In Jesus we will then be taken up into his divine life with his Father. In him we will love the Father and be loved by the Father. In other words, we will have eternal life, we will be living God's own life. In Jesus we will be partakers of the divine nature, we will be caught up into the mutual knowledge and love of the three divine persons in the Trinity.

b) By organic comparisons: While the social comparison of marriage gives us to see the wonderful person-to-person relationship we have with Jesus and with his Father, organic comparisons reveal the closeness of that relationship. Here then I would like to use the comparisons of the union of body and soul in man, the unity of Christ's humanity with his divinity and the comparison St. Paul uses for the Mystical Body of Christ.

Our body and soul certainly make up one living being, united in the most intimate way. Our rational soul seeks to live its life in our body, for only through our body can we, by our rational soul, see, hear and make things. But our body also wants to live its life through the soul, for, should the body desire some tasty food it must rely on the intelligence of the soul to direct it to that food or into cooking it.

It is much the same between Christ's humanity and his divinity. The divinity of Christ needed his humanity to teach mankind by word of mouth and to redeem the world by dying on the cross. But his humanity also needed his divinity in order to work miracles and utter prophecies. In these comparisons however, our body and Christ's humanity are not persons and hence such comparisons are not fully adequate.

The comparison St. Paul uses to explain Christ's Mystical Body has a special value for us here, in that it can help us to see the place Mary holds in our union with Jesus. St. Paul tells us that Jesus is the head of his Mystical Body, that the Church is his body , and the faithful are different members of his Body. Since, what the Church is externally, Mary is internally, when St. Paul says that the Church is Christ's body he is telling us that Mary is that body too.

Now Jesus, as the head of his Mystical Body is the source of its life and the director of all its activity. Therefore, whatever is done through Christ's body and its members, according to his will, are the actions of Jesus himself. But also, just as our body possesses all that its members can do, so Mary and the Church possess the fullness of all the gifts and graces Jesus has won for his body. The faithful, then, as members of that body: Mary and the Church, share in its fullness according to their different places and roles in the body.

Since however, the head, body and members make up but one living organic reality, Christ's Mystical Body, they all share in the total blessing of the whole even as all the members of our human body share in the well-being of the whole body as a human person. Or again, to use the social comparison of the family, all members share in the total good of the whole family and in the blessings proper to each one of its members.

Some aspects of our organic unity with Jesus: To better understand the nature of our organic unity with Jesus which is a unity of persons, there are several special aspects of this union I would like to consider.

First of all, we should know that there is only one other organic unity, besides our unity with Jesus in his Mystical Body, wherein the members are persons, and that unity is found between the three divine persons in the Trinity. Our Lord actually uses it as a comparison of our union with himself, "Father may they all be one: may they be one in us as you are in me and I am in you." (Jn. 17:21) Our unity with Jesus and with our fellow members in his Mystical Body is much like the unity of the three Divine Persons in the Trinity. We can state this in words but what the reality is like we have no way of knowing directly. However, there are a couple of considerations that can give us some added knowledge of what our unity with Jesus must be like.

The Holy Spirit, the Soul of the Mystical Body: The Holy Spirit is the source of our organic unity with Christ. Pope Pius XII in his encyclical on the Mystical Body, tells us that the Holy Spirit is the soul of the Mystical Body, that is, he is its principle of life and unity, even as he is the principle of life and unity of the three divine persons in the Trinity. Now God's divine life and nature cannot be multiplied and then be equally shared by several individuals, as our human nature and life can be multiplied and equally shared in by every individual human being. God's life is one and unique so that, we can share in it only by being united with its one living principle, much as the branch is united with the one life of the vine.

Now the living principle of God's divine life is the Holy Spirit, mutual love. For us to be united with God and participate in his life, the Holy Spirit must be the principle of our spiritual life just as the vine is the principle of the life in the branches. That is why St. Paul could say, "The love of God has been poured into our hearts by the Holy Spirit who has been given to us." (Rom. 5:5)

Through the Incarnation Christ's humanity was given to possess God's divine life through sanctifying grace. As we have seen in Part I (page 53), sanctifying grace has a created element and an uncreated element. Christ's humanity was adapted by the *created element* of sanctifying grace so as to be made capable of receiving God's divine life, the Holy Spirit, who is the *uncreated element* or reality given us in sanctifying grace. In this way, the Holy Spirit,

God's own divine life becomes the highest principle of life in Christ's humanity, much as our intellectual soul is the highest principle of life in our human nature or being, far superior to the animal life of our body.

When, therefore, we become one with Jesus by the new birth of Baptism, we are given as our higher principle of life the very life of God himself, the Holy Spirit, living in our head Jesus. Then Jesus, God, can live his divine life in us even as our soul lives its higher intellectual life in our animal body. All our actions, done in conformity with God's will, are the very actions of God, of Jesus, living in us through his Spirit.

Because the Holy Spirit — the mutual love of Father and Son — is the soul or principle of life in Christ's Mystical Body, all the members of Christ are united with God and with one another in and by the Holy Spirit. Hence, it is *in* the Holy Spirit that I love Mary and I am loved by Mary. It is *in* the Holy Spirit that, with Mary, I love Jesus and I am loved by Jesus. It is *in* the Holy Spirit that we love our fellow members and are loved by them. Wherever we find mutual love, the love of benevolence, there we find the Holy Spirit present and living. If as St Paul says, "Without the Holy Spirit we cannot proclaim that Jesus is Lord," how much more do we need the Holy Spirit for all our other acts of faith and love.

Union with Jesus in Self-Consciousness: In our organic unity with Jesus in the divine life **Jesus and we** are both persons-unlike our body in its union with our soul. But how are persons united in an organic unity? The only answer must be, by becoming one in self-consciousness. That is how the three divine person are united in the Trinity.

In God, whatever pertains to the divine nature is common to all three persons. But self-consciousness pertains to the *nature of a being* and hence, the three divine persons can have but one self-consciousness. That is why Jesus could say to Philip, "Do you not believe that I am in the Father and the Father in me?" (Jn. 14:10)

We cannot imagine what it must be like for two persons to have the same self-consciousness, but perhaps we can get an inkling of what it is like by considering the marital act in marriage. In this act of human love, husband and wife want to become so one that there is no separateness between them, and indeed, they actually experience something of that in the peak moment of the marital act wherein they seem to be merged into one another, into one self-consciousness. If they could make that peak moment to last forever, it would appear to them as being the summit of human happiness. What will it be like then to be so united in self-consciousness with God, with Jesus, with Mary and with all the angels and saints in heaven?

We can find a certain confirmation of this in the mystics. St. John of the Cross speaks of a mystical experience which he calls "A substantial touch" wherein the substance of the soul seems to become one with the very substance of God. This is also confirmed by what theologians tell us concerning the Beatific Vision, which we will enjoy in heaven. We cannot know God as he is in himself by any intellectual image, for no created image can represent God. Therefore, God himself must take the place of that created image. In that case we will know God much as we know ourselves by a self-conscious experience of being God. Indeed, some individuals have experienced a oneness with God even in this life and found they could only explain it by saying, "I am God" to the shock, if not the scandal, of their hearers. Truly God has willed to make us gods insofar as that is possible for us as creatures to receive.

B) WHAT WE SHARE IN JESUS AND MARY

Since we are called to share in all the gifts and blessings of Jesus and Mary, much as a child shares in the gifts and blessings of his parents, or, as a branch in all the fruitfulness of the vine, let us see what these blessings are that Jesus and Mary have to share with us.

l. What we share in Jesus: By the Incarnation Jesus took to himself our humanity. Therefore, all that God conferred on the humanity of Jesus we share in, as being living members of that humanity. Since the humanity of Jesus received the person of the Son of God, we, in some way, share in his person so that St. Paul could write, "You are all one person in Christ." (Gal. 3:28) If we are one person with Christ then we too are God's sons, his adopted sons in Christ. But "If sons, then also heirs of God and co-heirs of Christ, sharing in his sufferings so as to share his glory." (Rom. 8:17) Christ's humanity was also given to share in God's divine life through sanctifying grace. Therefore, that life becomes our life even as the life of the vine becomes the life of the branches.

Not only do we share in what God has given Jesus in his humanity, we also share in all that Jesus has won for his humanity and hence, for us, his members, through his mortal life and sacrificial death on earth. So true is this that St. Thomas Aquinas says, "All the satisfactions and merits Jesus has won through his passion and death and resurrection belong to Jesus and to us, his members, in the same way as it would belong to a man, who, being what Jesus is, performed those same works." (cf. Sum. III,48,1) If that is true of all Jesus' satisfactions and merits, it is also true of all his virtues: his humility, obedience, patience, charity, and all his acts of adoration, thanksgiving, reparation and petition to God. These are all ours in Jesus and therefore, we, his members can freely use them as our own to supply for all we ourselves may lack. In Jesus we have died to sin, we have risen in him to a new life and we have ascended into heaven with him and are now seated with him at the right hand of the Father in glory. Death will simply rend the veil that now keeps us from seeing and enjoying all this.

2. What we share in Mary: As Jesus unites us perfectly with the Father in divine friendship so Mary unites us perfectly with Jesus in human friendship. And just like Jesus, Mary shares with us, her children, everything she has received and won through her perfect union with Jesus in human friendship. A mother cannot fail to share with her children all she has received from her husband and won from him through her love. Since Mary lived with Jesus a human life of perfect friendship as his spouse in the order of grace, she shares with us, her children, all that she has received from Jesus and all that she has won from him through her faithful love.

Of the gifts she has received from God the first is the privilege of her Immaculate Conception. That we will share in this privilege of Mary is quite evident from what St. Paul says about the Church, "Jesus made her glorious without spot or wrinkle or anything like that, but wholly faultless." (Eph. 5:27) Since these words are true only of Mary as an individual, when St. Paul applies them to the Church he is telling us that Mary and the Church are one and that we, as members of the Church, share in all the gifts and graces of Mary.

Another gift and privilege of Mary is her divine motherhood. In that privilege we share through baptism, wherein we give Jesus our humanity so that he may live in us his human life of love for his Father. In doing so, we give birth to Jesus in ourselves, in one of the members of his humanity, and, in so doing, we are as his mother in this limited sense. Again, Mary is the perfect spouse of Jesus. When we unite ourselves with Mary in striving to live with Jesus his life of love for his Father, Mary shares with us, her children, her own perfect unity with Jesus as his spouse.

As with Jesus so too with Mary, we share not only in her gifts, but also in her holiness, that is, in all she has acquired by her faithful living of the gifts she has received from God. Since she did that to the highest possible perfection, Christ's active redemption has achieved in Mary the highest possible fruit or effect: perfect passive redemption. All that Mary has thus acquired, she lovingly shares with all her children to the extent that we freely come to her for help in our striving to live with Jesus his life of love for his Father.

As Jesus, so also Mary, shares with us all her virtues and her acts of adoration, thanksgiving, reparation and petitions. Her perfect "Fiat" to the divine will becomes ours; her perfect correspondence to God's will throughout her whole life she shares with us. She willingly unites us with herself in her total gift of herself with Jesus to his Father. And all the glory and happiness that is now hers in heaven she longs to share with us when our mortal life is over.

That we can so share in all that Jesus and Mary have and are, flows from the reality of our organic unity with them through sanctifying grace. All the members of the human body share in the total well-being of the body and in the blessings each member contributes to the body. And so it is with us in Christ's Mystical Body. But since our unity therein is between persons it will be a unity in self-consciousness. We will share in all the blessings of Jesus and Mary and the saints, as though we were actually they themselves.

In faith we must believe that we possess all the riches of Jesus and Mary as being our very own. Not only will we rejoice in eternity as being united with God through the riches of Jesus and Mary, but even now, in this life, we can use their riches as our own, can merit by them and, in this way, we can enter ever more fully into their reward.

By using, as my own, all the merits and riches of Mary I can be united with Jesus in perfect human friendship. By using, as my own, all the merits and riches of Jesus I can be united with the

Father in perfect divine friendship even as was Jesus when on earth. Nothing can please God more than when we so use all he has given us in Jesus and Mary in order to come to him. Indeed, it was his great love for us that moved him to give them to us that through them we might be united with him in the highest possible way.

3. Living the Truth: When we seek everything in what God has made Jesus and Mary to be to us, we are living the greatest and most fundamental truth of creation, namely, that the creator is the only source of every good and that the creature has nothing it has not received from its creator. Sanctity is humility, living the truth, for that alone is real. Hence, the more perfectly we seek everything in God and not in ourselves, then we are living the truth more fully and the greater is our sanctity and union with God in loving friendship.

As St. Paul tells us, "We do not have to go up to heaven to bring Christ down nor go down into the depths to bring him up; we have only to believe that God raised Jesus from the dead and we shall be saved, (cf Rom. 10:6-9) We have only to accept all that God is giving us in Jesus and Mary with faith, hope and love. We must believe that it is real; we must trust that if we strive to keep our wills in conformity with God's will, we will certainly obtain everything God has promised us in Jesus and Mary in spite of every obstacle and setback. Above all, we must love God by esteeming what he is giving us in Jesus and Mary and by keeping our habitual will always centered on doing his will.

C) HOW WE SHOULD LIVE SO AS TO SHARE IN THE PERFECTION OF JESUS AND MARY

Through Jesus and Mary God is calling us to a share in his divine life by a unity that approaches identity. It is a spiritual unity that is more real than any created unity we can experience in this world. It is a unity that is made possible only through Jesus, the God-man, who is our sole mediator with God.

While our call to share in God's divine life is a wholly gratuitous gift of God, still there is something we must do, even though it is as nothing compared to what God is freely offering us. First of all we must know about the gift that he is offering to us; then, we must freely accept it; and finally we must freely live the reality or the demands of that gift.

Now the reason or goal for accepting God's gift of friendship with himself is **twofold**: our own personal perfection and happiness, that is, our own salvation and sanctification; and secondly: the salvation and sanctification of all mankind with whom we form one social and organic reality.

Here then, I wish first to give a clear explanation of this twofold goal for which we should accept God's offer of friendship and then how we should live with Jesus, in this life: first **as man** and then **as God**, so as to share most fully in God's divine friendship. I will also explain what determines the degree to which each individual will share in the total perfection of Jesus and Mary.

1. Our twofold goal in accepting God's offer of friendship: Man is an individual but he is also social. He cannot find his own personal fulfillment and happiness without a relationship of mutual knowledge and love with another intellectual being, primarily with God, but also with other intellectual beings like himself. Hence, while man must seek his own salvation and sanctification in God, he must also work for the salvation and sanctification of all mankind.

Man's personal goal; his salvation: To accept God's offer of friendship is something wholly personal to ourselves; no one can make that act of acceptance for us. Therefore, our salvation and sanctification is essentially something between God and ourselves. It consists in our acceptance of his friendship and in the degree to which we freely live what that acceptance requires. If I accept a friend as being everything to me, I will want to be always with him, at least in mind and spirit. I will tend to seek everything I need from him as though needing no other source. My one desire will be to please him as my greatest joy by doing all I can to fulfill his every wish and desire. I will be so intent on his good and happiness that no sacrifice or suffering will be too great in order to please him. Is not that how husband and wife love one another? How much more then should we so love God?

b. Man's social goal; the salvation of all mankind: We must also seek the salvation and sanctification of all mankind: all our fellow brothers and sisters in Christ's Mystical Body. Mankind forms one social reality, as we have seen, for we cannot really know ourselves nor possess the fullness of our humanity without a sharing in the individual gifts of every other human being. Hence, while our own fulfillment and happiness consists in a union of friendship with God through Jesus, we also need to be united with all mankind, with all our brothers and sisters in their union of friendship with God. Because of our need of them, their salvation and sanctification must be of great concern for us both as contributing to our own fullness of happiness but especially because there is nothing more pleasing to God, our beloved, than their salvation. If we really love God , we will seek to give him the greatest joy possible, but there is nothing God desires more than the salvation and sanctification of all mankind. Hence, we must long to bring all our brothers and sisters to the same goal of happiness as ourselves.

As we know, God willed to save mankind from within: and first of all through the Incarnation. God willed that his divine Son should become one of our human race, its new head and leader. He is the new Adam, complete in his social nature as man with Mary, the new Eve. Being complete as man, God willed that Jesus should win our salvation with Mary's consent and cooperation through his supreme sacrifice on Calvary.

So also now, God has willed to dispense the saving grace of Christ's salvation to individual men and women down the ages only through the cooperation of the living members of Christ's Mystical Body. As our soul cannot act in the physical order except through our body, so Jesus does not will to dispense his saving grace to those living in the world today except through the free cooperation of the visible members of his Mystical Body. God has thus willed to need our cooperation to promote the continuing of mankind's salvation in the world today. If we fail to do our part, God will not be able to save all men and women as he desires. While this is a great privilege for us it is also a grave responsibility, requiring our fidelity and generosity.

If you ask, why God has willed to act in this way, the answer must be because he wants us, his living members, to grow in charity and merit. Jesus, Mary and the saints, being now in glory, can no longer grow in charity and merit, for they have reached their final state of growth. But we who are still in this world can grow in charity and merit by using all their grace and merits as our own by reason of our unity in Christ's Mystical Body.

That God has actually willed to need our cooperation in saving souls appears quite evident in the lives of some mystics. Jesus asked them to give him their good works and sufferings in order to save sinners, not only in general, but at times even for some particular person. We also find Mary in her apparitions asking her children for their prayers and sacrifices that she might hold back God's just anger from striking the world. Thus, even Mary, who is said to be omnipotent by her supplications, cannot dispense grace without the cooperation of her children on earth. We can only explain this need on the assumption that God has willed to need the cooperation of the living members of his Mystical Body for the dispensing of his saving grace.

Since it is always Jesus who acts through his members, when we freely cooperate with him, we enter into a share of Jesus' own charity and merit. In this way Jesus, as it were, comes to the full stature of his Mystical Body: his members enter into the full life and merits of Jesus himself, their head. The more our actions, therefore, proceed from the Spirit of Jesus living within us, the more they are the actions of Jesus and the more they share in the merits of Jesus himself and the more effective they are in contributing to the salvation of other souls.

Two ways we can contribute to the salvation of others: Now there are two ways we can cooperate with Jesus in the salvation of our fellow members in Christ's Mystical Body: one **external** and the other **internal**. That we can cooperate externally is quite evident in the ministerial works of the Church, especially in the dispensation of the sacraments. One cannot receive the sacraments of the Eucharist and of Penance without the ministry of an ordained priest. But this external way of helping others is not limited to ordained priests. Every Christian can contribute externally in bringing Christ's saving grace to others by teaching, counseling, and good example. The need of such external cooperation is very evident in St. Paul's words, "They will not believe unless they have heard, and they will not hear unless they have a preacher, and they will not have a preacher unless someone is sent." (Rom. 10:14-15)

Internally we can help save souls through prayers, sacrifices and good works. Since it is really Jesus who lives and acts in us, his members, such prayers and good works partake of the charity and merits of Jesus himself. They thus have the value and efficacy of being the actions of Jesus himself living in his members. That is why St. James could write, "The prayers of a just man availeth much before God." (Jm. 5:16)

This internal way of helping souls is far more important than the external way. Indeed all external acts, outside the efficacy of the sacraments, have no value in saving souls unless accompanied by some meritorious internal motivation. In order to produce a supernatural effect you need a supernatural cause. Hence, unless the external action is accompanied by some good internal motive or prayer either of oneself or someone else, such actions can produce no supernatural fruit in others. While this internal efficacy of our prayers and good works may not be visible, it is still very real. The Church has always recognized this, as is quite evident, in the fact that she has made St. Therese of Lisieux the co-patron of the missions together with St. Francis Xavier. It is said that this Carmelite saint saved as many souls by her hidden life in Carmel as St. Francis did through his missionary activity coupled, indeed, with his own interior life of prayer and sacrifice.

c. Some related problems: We may ask, "If God has willed to need the cooperation of the living members of his Mystical Body in the dispensing of his saving grace, what place do Mary and the saints have in dispensing grace?" While it is certain that Mary and the saints can pray and intercede with God for us, still in what their help actually consists is shrouded in mystery. It would appear that they can inspire us with good thoughts and desires so as to move us to acts of virtue and good works, but for the grace actually to perform those good works we must either pray ourselves, or others for us, in order to win the necessary grace. Perhaps it is the faith and fervor of love with which we ourselves or others ask Mary and the saints for their help that determines the measure of what they can obtain from God. Was not even Jesus limited in working miracles by the measure of the individual's faith?

That God needs our prayers and those of others may explain the difficulty some have with those words of Scripture, "God never tries us beyond our strength." (1 Cor. 10:13) This statement may be true on the condition that either the person himself or others pray for the grace one needs to endure such trials. Since God will never refuse to answer such a prayer, the trial is indeed never beyond one's personal capacity, provided he does what is in his power, namely, to pray for the strength.

Another question one may have is, "Why pray to the saints when we can pray directly to Jesus himself?" Well, all prayers are really directed to God or Jesus, but we can ask Mary and the saints to present them to Jesus for us so that through their favor with Jesus our petitions will carry greater weight. It is also an act of honoring God in his saints which is very pleasing to God. However, in whatever way it is that we obtain God's grace, it will always remain true that the grace itself will be imparted to us through the maternal mediation of Mary.

Can all souls be saved: Since God has willed that his saving grace should be applied to mankind only as merited by living members of his Mystical Body, what is the possibility of all souls being saved? There are many people in the world who are not disposed to perceive any divine inspiration coming from God or the saints, nor are they inclined to pray for God's grace. Hence, they must depend on the prayers and good works of others for those special graces needed for their salvation. Here we see how much God depends on the zeal and generous love of his faithful children.

In a private revelation Jesus once said to a Canadian nun, "If all religious were what they should be, all other souls would be saved." And we can rightly add, "If all Christians were what they should be, all other souls would be saved." Another saintly person asked Jesus, "Is it possible that all who are living on earth today could be saved?" Jesus answered, "All things are possible through the merits and Name of Jesus Christ."

If the faithful are generous in prayers and good works, there is nothing they cannot do through the merits of Jesus in winning souls for eternal life. Although it is true that God gives sufficient grace to all for their salvation, and that no one is lost but through his own stubborn refusal to accept God's offer of friendship, still others could win for them those special graces whereby they would be moved to turn to God in love and sorrow. Realizing this, and knowing how much we have failed to be generous with God in the past, we may wonder how we will be able to face God at the end of life, should some soul be lost who could have been saved had we been more generous? Is there any way we can make up for these failures of the past now that we recognize what was lost by them? Yes, there is, as I will show later, for there is nothing Jesus cannot do or make right if we go to him in faith and love.

2. How we should live a life of friendship with Jesus as man in this life: In explaining how we should live a life of friendship with Jesus **as man** in this life, there are two social comparisons I would like to use: first that of the family and secondly that of the more intimate union of spousal love between husband and wife. The comparison of the family will help us see how we should live the beginning, as it were, of our life of friendship with Jesus, and that of spouses its more perfect final form. For an organic comparison I would like to use that of the vine and its branches.

a. The social comparison of the family: Before, in explaining the nature of our friendship with Jesus as man, I used the comparison of the family and likened Jesus and Mary to being our parents and we their children: forming one loving family. As their children they love us even as they love themselves, and hence, there is nothing they will not do for us or share with us. However, even they are limited in what they can do for us by reason of our free response to their solicitude. What that free response should be is well exemplified by the way of Spiritual Childhood as given in the Gospel and rediscovered by St. Therese of Lisieux.

First of all our response requires a deep humility. We, as creatures, are more poor and weak before God than any child before its parents. But it is just its weakness and poverty that assures the child, and hence, ourselves, of sharing in all the wealth and power of Jesus and Mary. Although we are adults in the physical order, in the spiritual order, we are weak and poor and ignorant before God.

In our spiritual relationship with God, however, we generally tend to act like the two-year-old who, not knowing his parents, tries to make his own way in the world. No wonder, like that child, we are full of worry, fear and anxiety. Should such a child suddenly come to discover its parents and their desire to care for him, all his fears and worries would vanish and he would then experience that happy freedom so characteristic of childhood. So it is that we must come to find all our spiritual fulfillment in Jesus and Mary. That is why God so often lets us experience our weakness and emptiness. God wants us to become as little children, but he does not want us to become childish. We must not imitate the ignorance and levity of children but those virtues that well-befit their total dependence on their parents.

First of all we must have faith: we must believe that God, that Jesus and Mary are real and that they love us more than any parents could ever love their children. We must also believe they have the power and the desire to love and care for us in the most perfect way. When our faith is strong, we will then go to Jesus and Mary with that simple and secure confidence of a little child which so wins the hearts of its loving parents. Seeing how good and loving Jesus is to us, we will love him as the best of Fathers and, indeed, as our greatest and supreme good. We will freely abandon ourselves completely into his loving arms, knowing that everything he arranges for us by his loving providence has to be for our greatest good, even though, to us, it may seem otherwise. Like a little child we will rest secure and happy in the loving care of Jesus, content just to love him as our Father who is everything to us. Nothing pleases Jesus more than such simple childlike trust and love. Then too, we will be inspired by zeal; seeing and experiencing how wonderful our Father is, we will want all our brothers and sisters to know and love and experience his goodness even as we do.

Mary, being our mother, loves us in the same way as Jesus, and she is also our model. As a creature, she lived the Little Way of Spiritual Childhood most perfectly before us, so much so, that she became the spouse of Jesus. Parents, in raising their children, want them to come to the fullness of perfect adulthood even as themselves. A woman who loves her husband as her own greatest joy and treasure would desire, were that possible, that her child should grow and love him even as she does and become his spouse. Of course in the human order that is not possible but in the spiritual order with Jesus it is. That is why, in our union of friendship with Jesus as man, we must also come to love him as our spouse, in likeness to Mary.

b. The social comparison of spouses: Loving Jesus as our spouse is necessary in order to reach that highest social fulfillment of our nature which wants to know and to be known, to love and to be loved by someone who is essentially equal to ourselves. The friendship between parents and child is not wholly equal even though it is on the intellectual level. But between husband and wife it is basically equal, although even here, the husband has a certain precedence. The husband, being the more dominant and leader, is the first to give himself in love to his wife, who, on receiving his love, gives herself back to him in a return of love. They compliment one another, thus achieving that most basic social need of mutual knowing and loving. They need one another for their full human happiness, as is quite evident, should one of them die.

In much the same way we need to live with Jesus, as man, in the likeness of being his spouse. Through the Incarnation Jesus has truly made himself our equal in nature so that as man, he needs us for his own human happiness and we need him, even more so, for our human happiness. He is the bridegroom and we his bride; he is the male and we are as the female in our relation with him. As such we compliment each other even as do husband and wife.

Being united with Jesus as his spouse, we must live a life of loving friendship with him in the likeness of husband and wife, in the likeness of bridegroom and bride. His part, as bridegroom, is to sustain and strengthen his bride while our part, as his bride, is to comfort him by our tender love and perfect confidence. Since we, as creatures, are as nothing before him, our part is to receive everything from him and then return it all back to him enriched with our personal love. To that end we must see every good as coming to us from Jesus, as a gift of his love: all the beauties and marvels of nature, all the joys found in human friendships, and above all, the supernatural gift of sanctifying grace with all that goes with it: the gift of faith, the Church, the sacraments, especially the Eucharist. Our gratitude for all these gifts will be unbounded; we will not think of seeking anything in ourselves or in creatures apart from God or contrary to his will. If we did that, we would deeply wound his heart, as would a wife who should seek in herself or in others what her husband could and desired to do for her far more perfectly. We will rejoice to use all his riches to make up for anything we may lack, adorning ourselves with all his gifts, so as to make ourselves more beautiful and pleasing in his sight.

We will try to return everything back to Jesus, enriched with our love, by using them to fulfill his every wish and desire. But at the same time we will want to be united with him, living in his presence all the day long, in so far as that is possible. We will seek to please him more than ourselves, for we will find our joy more in making him happy than in our own happiness. We will accept his will in every providential event with loving trust and abandonment, cooperating therein as fully as we can. In all our problems and difficulties we will go to him for light and strength. Should we cause him any pain by some fault or failure we will come to him in loving sorrow more concerned with relieving his pain than our own shame and humiliation. We will seek to make reparation for the pain so many sinners give him by loving him all the more and by making little sacrifices to prove our love.

It is here that devotion to the Sacred Heart of Jesus has its deepest and most appropriate place. Jesus has a real human heart like ours and hence, he needs our human love for his own human happiness, even as we need to experience his divine love coming from a human heart. God, in Jesus, has willed to need our love so that we might have the joy of really giving him something in return for his great love for us: that we might even love him as much as he loves us.

c. Using an organic comparison: When we consider our union with Jesus as man as being organic, the comparison of the vine and branch is quite appropriate. In living a life of human friendship with Jesus we have one and the same life, like the vine and the branch. The more fully the branch is joined to the life of the vine the greater is its fruitfulness. The more fully we are united with Jesus in his life of sanctifying grace, the more fully we will share in all his riches and merits. So long as our actions are according to the will of Jesus they are the actions of Jesus, and so produce a divine fruit worthy of eternal life. Thus our union with Jesus in loving friendship is far more real than any social comparison can convey; we truly possess one organic life with Jesus, the very life of God through sanctifying grace.

In living a life of friendship with Jesus as man, we must first of all live with him according to the virtues of Spiritual Childhood, and then those virtues proper to the union of spousal love. Since Mary has lived such a life with Jesus, as man, in the most perfect possible way, both as his child and as his bride, we can do nothing better than to ask Mary to unite us with herself in going to Jesus. Mary will be most happy to do so and Jesus will be delighted to receive us as coming to him in the loving arms of Mary. Mary will also be happy to adorn us with all her own supreme virtues. That is why we cannot be more perfectly united with Jesus as man, than through Mary.

3. How we should live a life of friendship with Jesus as God in this life: Our union of friendship with Jesus **as God** is not really distinct from our union of friendship with him as man; they are just two aspects of one perfect friendship. We do not go to Jesus first as man, through Mary, and then to the Father through Jesus as God, somewhat as one takes a car to the airport, and there leaves it, to take the plane to his final destination. It is more like a child who, uniting itself with its mother, is taken up into her arms and presented by her to its Father. Mary always remains indispensable in our union with Jesus, both as man and as God. As we become united with Jesus in loving friendship as man through Mary, we are at the same time taken up with Jesus through Mary into his life of friendship with his Father.

In order to understand what we must do on our part to be united with Jesus as God in his divine life, we will need to use the social comparison of husband and wife and how they seek their **twofold** higher natural goals. Husband and wife, even while seeking their mutual happiness in one another, must still seek the higher goal of a loving **friendship with God** and of procuring the **well-being of their family** both in the present and for the future. So it is that in our friendship with Jesus we must still seek the higher goal of being united with Jesus in his **friendship with his Father**, and the well-being and **salvation of all our fellow members** in Jesus' Mystical Body.

Here I will first consider the social comparison of how husband and wife work together for their twofold higher goals, and then apply it to how we must live with Jesus his higher life of friendship with his Father so as to procure our twofold higher goals. Then I will use a couple of organic comparisons to help us understand the closeness of our union with Jesus as God.

a. The social comparison of how husband and wife seek their higher goals: Although husband and wife seek a mutual happiness in one another, that happiness is limited because perfect happiness can only be found in a union of friendship with someone who is all truth and goodness, namely, God. Hence, in living their lives together they must, at the same time, mutually help one another to become more united with God in his divine life of friendship.

How husband and wife must live for God: In living for God, the husband and wife should help one another to know God, for we cannot love what we do not know. They will, then, be attentive in seeing God and his goodness in all his works: in all the blessings they enjoy in creation, in the beauty of their children, in their relationships with other people and especially in God's gift of themselves to each other. They will seek to know God and his goodness still more by reading and studying his divine revelation in the Bible.

They will try to show their love for God and their gratitude to him by offering tithes to maintain and promote worship in his Church, and in alleviating the needs of the poor. They will love and honor God by praying and worshiping him together, and as members of the community of the faithful. They will prove their love still more by striving always to do God's will as it come to them through civil and Church authority, the duties of their state in life, and the arrangements of God's loving providence. They will help each other to understand God's love for them in trials and sufferings, knowing that, as a loving Father, he allows such trials, not for our harm but for our greater spiritual growth. They will love all God's children, their fellow men and women, even as they love Jesus himself, by doing all they can to help them both materially and spiritually.

How husband and wife must live for their families: At the same time husband and wife will not neglect their other higher goal: the well-being of their family both in the present and for the future. Since they love their children as themselves, their children will be caught up into their own mutual love for each other and in their love for God. Hence, they will willingly make any sacrifice for the true well-being of their children, both material and spiritual.

In so working for the well-being of their family and children, husband and wife compliment one another, both seeking the same goal, but each in his own different way. The husband, as the principal authority and provider, works to obtain the necessities for his family. The wife, using all that he provides, seeks to establish a loving home and cares for the needs of their children. The husband is happy when his wife uses all he earns in the most generous and prudent way for the welfare of the family. And the wife is happy with all he provides so that she can give him and their children a beautiful home-life full of happiness. However, the husband would be grieved if, while he was earning more than enough, his wife were stingy in the use of it for the family and even in helping others.

b. How we should seek our higher goals in likeness to husband and wife: Let us now apply the above comparison to ourselves to see how we should live a life of loving friendship with Jesus, as God, in order to achieve our twofold higher goal: our own happiness and salvation and the salvation of all mankind.

1) Seeking our own happiness and Salvation: As husband and wife seek their higher happiness in helping each other in being united with God in mutual knowledge and love, so we must become more conscious of our union in mutual knowledge and love with God through Jesus. We must do it first through faith in what we find revealed in the Gospel and then through love, by living what we thus believe.

Living in mutual knowledge with God: As for mutual knowledge with God we can be sure that the Father knows us even as he knows his Son, Jesus. When Jesus says, "No one knows the Son but the Father," we too are included in the Father's knowledge of his Son. And when Jesus says, "No one knows the Father but the Son and to whom the Son chooses to reveal him, we can be sure that Jesus gives us to know his Father even as he himself knows the Father. (cf. Mt. 11: 27)

Indeed, by knowing Jesus we also know the Father, for as Jesus has said, "He who sees me sees the Father." (Jn. 14:9) Since we are known by the Father in Jesus we are therefore never alone. Jesus said to his disciples, "You will leave me alone and yet I am not alone for the Father is always with Me." (Jn. 16:32) Hence, like Jesus himself, we are forever embraced in the Father's knowledge and love, which are ineffable and divine and eternally present.

Living in mutual love with God: Just as through Jesus we are united with the Father in mutual knowledge, so too, in mutual love. We must believe that we are loved by the Father even as Jesus himself is loved by the Father. As Jesus said, "The Father himself loves you for loving me and believing that I came from God." (Jn. 16:27)

And Jesus longs to unite us with himself in his own love for the Father. Hence, those words, "Father I have made your name known to them...so that the love with which you love me may be in them and so that I may be in them." (Jn. 17: 26) Jesus wants to live in us so that we can love the Father even as Jesus loves the Father and that the Father will love us even as he loves Jesus. "Anyone who loves me will be loved by my Father and I shall love him and show myself to him." (Jn. 14:21) And again, "If anyone loves me he will keep my words and My Father will love him and we shall come to him and make our home with him." (Jn. 14:23) If the Father loves us even as he loves Jesus, then he will share everything he has with us even as with Jesus himself. And so it is, for Jesus has said, "Whatever the Father has is mine." (Jn. 16:15) And, as the father of the prodigal son said to his elder son, so Jesus says to us. "My son you are always with me and all I have is yours." (Lk. 15:31) All the Father has Jesus has, and all Jesus has he shares with us.

Proving our love by doing God's will: Seeing how much the Father loves us in Jesus we will seek to make a return of love in union with Jesus. This we will do with Jesus by always seeking to do the Father's will by keeping his commandments. We will be mindful of those words, "If you keep my commandments you will remain in my love even as I have kept my Father's commandments and remain in his love." (Jn. 15:10) Doing the Father's will, as a proof of our love, will be our greatest desire. We will want to say with Jesus, "I always do the things that please him." (Jn. 8:29) And, "My food is to do the will of him who sent me." (Jn. 4:34) Indeed, so great will be our desire to prove our love for the Father that we will willingly unite ourselves with Jesus in his supreme act of self-donation and sacrifice on Calvary; "Sharing his sufferings that we might share his glory." (cf. Rom. 8:17)

Proving our love by living the virtues: Love is also expressed in the practice of the virtues, especially those proper to a creature before its creator. One of the most important of these is humility. United with Jesus as man we will humble ourselves before his Father saying, "The Father is greater than I." (Jn. 14:28) And also, "The Son can do nothing by himself, he can only do what he sees the Father doing." (Jn. 5:19) And, "It is the Father living in me who is doing this work." (Jn. 14:10)

Seeing how much we have been given in Jesus our gratitude will know no bounds, especially in seeing God's preference for those who are poor and weak. Our hearts will echo those words of Jesus, "I thank you Father for hiding these things from the learned and the clever and revealing them to mere children." (Lk. 10:21)

Experiencing the unfailing care of the Father's love for us, our trust will be so strong that with Jesus we will be able to say, "Father I thank you for hearing my prayer: I know that you always hear me." (Jn. 11:41-42)

But above all we will rejoice to prove our love by our complete abandonment to his loving will and providence even in the face of the greatest suffering, repeating Jesus' own words, "My Father, if this cup cannot pass me without my drinking it, your will be done." (Mt. 26:42) By so living with Jesus, his life of love for his Father, in this world, we will be caught up with Jesus in his eternal life of mutual knowledge and love with his Father. We will be living the life of the Trinity here on earth.

2) Promoting the Father's kingdom: In taking us to himself as his bride, Jesus has introduced us into the divine family of God as a member or subject of his eternal kingdom. Being now a subject of that kingdom we must seek to promote its well-being even as Jesus does. Now the well-being of that kingdom consists in the salvation and sanctification of all its members, so that, in the end, we may all share in the beauty and happiness of the whole kingdom together with the particular beauty and goodness of each and every individual member. All will be like a beautiful and well-arranged garden where every flower has its particular beauty while at the same time contributing to the over-all beauty of God's heavenly garden.

As I mentioned before, God has willed that his saving grace should be applied to mankind by the living members of Christ Mystical Body. Jesus has provided all that is necessary for the salvation of mankind and now we, as his bride or wife, must freely take and apply all this wealth, he has put into our hands, to promote the well-being of his kingdom. In this way we are called to compliment Jesus much as a wife compliments her husband in promoting the well-being of their family.

Being generous in using Christ's riches: Since Jesus has put his infinite riches at our disposal, we should use them in the most generous possible way. Jesus loves every soul, even as parents love all their children, and so he seeks their salvation and sanctification with infinite love. As his bride, we must share in his love for souls as something most pleasing to him. As a queen who seeks to love her beloved, the king, all the more tenderly in order to obtain all she desires from him, so we must seek to love Jesus in order to win from him all the favors we desire for souls. Knowing the generosity of Jesus' own heart and all the riches he has put at our disposal, we will be most generous in asking and using all his riches for the salvation of souls. Surely Jesus delights to see that the heart of his bride is perfectly attuned to his own loving and magnanimous heart.

One time a holy person offered Jesus a task she was doing for the salvation of two souls, and Jesus quickly retorted, "Only two, not a hundred, not a thousand?" Jesus can do more than we can imagine. Hence, we should not hesitate to ask for anything we feel inspired to ask, even if it should appear impossible to us. Like a little child, who judges that his father can do anything, we will let our hearts direct our requests rather than our mind. And we can be sure that God can and wants to give us far more than we know how to ask. Hence, we should not hesitate to ask him for what appears impossible to us, leaving it up to him to figure out how to fulfill our request. That is what St. Therese of Lisieux did with some of her impossible desires and she was not disappointed.

Mary the first in winning grace: Here I would like to add a little point of interest. Mary, in the order of grace, but not in the order of time, was the first to win the application of Christ's saving grace for other souls. Mary alone on Calvary retained faith in Jesus as the Messiah. Hence, she alone was disposed, through that faith, to receive the grace of salvation at that moment. But once Jesus had died, he could no longer merit. Therefore, Mary was, in this special sense, the only living member of Christ on earth who could win the application of his saving grace for other souls, that is, for the apostles and the early Christians. Only then could they, in their turn, win Christ's saving grace for others, and so on down the ages. Here we see that, as Mary's consent was necessary for Jesus to become man and for him to save us on Calvary, so Mary's cooperation was necessary so that the fruits of Christ's salvation could begin to be applied to all mankind down the ages. This is surely another reason for Mary's title to being the Mediatrix of all graces.

c. An organic comparison of how we should live with Jesus as God: The social comparisons I have used show us how we should live with Jesus his life of friendship with his Father in pursuing the goal of our salvation and that of all our fellow members in Jesus. Using an organic comparison can help us better understand the close intimacy Jesus desires to have with us in so living for God and for others.

The comparison I would like to use is the unity which exists between our soul and our body. Our intellectual soul so needs our body that it cannot act in the physical world without it. And our body needs our spiritual soul even more, for without the soul, our body is dead. In much the same way we are united with Jesus. Jesus needs us and we need him. He cannot act or will not act in the physical world of souls except through the members of his Mystical Body. Hence, he needs us to save souls. If we are not united with him through sanctifying grace, he cannot act through us. If we are united with him in grace, but choose to follow our own will instead of his, our actions are merely human.

It is here that the comparison of a horse and its rider is helpful. When the horse is perfectly submissive to the guidance of its rider, it becomes as one with the rider in achieving the rider's higher goal, even though the horse can have no knowledge of that higher goal. So it is when we are perfectly docile to the Spirit of Jesus living in us that Jesus can accomplish divine works through us, although we have no way of knowing them except to a limited extent through faith. What Jesus can do through us in this way is seen in some of the saints like St. Paul, St. Francis Xavier, and today in Mother Theresa. Indeed, as Jesus has said, "We will do even greater works than he did himself." (cf. Jn. 14:12) The reason for that is because it is really Jesus himself who is acting in us his members. What Jesus can do in us is only limited by our free cooperation. What would our world be like if everyone allowed Jesus to live fully in them? We would have an anticipated heaven on earth.

d. Some consequences of our union with Jesus as God: Through our union with Jesus as God, we can accomplish things we would never imagine possible. Let us consider some off these.

Jesus can supply for all we lack: If we can use the riches and merits of Jesus as our own in applying them for the salvation of others we can also use them to supply for whatever we lack in the way of our own sanctification. Surely a husband desires that his wife should use all his riches to beautify and perfect herself so that he might find still greater joy in her beauty and goodness. Therefore, while we sincerely strive for our spiritual growth and perfection, we should not worry about our weakness and involuntary faults and failures. We can trust Jesus to make up for all we lack. Surely nothing pleases Jesus more than when we come to him in loving humility and trust, knowing that he can and will make right everything that is wanting in us. Do not parents rejoice when their children come to them in all their needs. They would be disappointed if their child were so perfect as never to need their help and forgiveness. Hence, we can ask Jesus to make up for everything we lack in going to his Father and we can ask Mary to make up for everything we lack in going to Jesus.

What I have just said does not apply to deliberate faults in the same way as to faults of frailty. Deliberate faults contain a lack of love and so wound the heart of Jesus. But still, even after such faults, if we come back to Jesus in loving sorrow and repentance, he will forgive and restore us to his love more fully than did the father in the case of his prodigal son.

Redeeming the past: By trusting Jesus to make up for all we lack, we can even redeem the past – those times when, not knowing and loving God sufficiently, we lived only for ourselves and caused him so much pain and sorrow. When we think of all these failures and, especially that some souls might be lost because of them, we may feel deeply distressed and wish we could find some way to redeem that part of our past. Through Jesus we can do just that.

Since our sanctification is really God's work in us, with our consent, there is nothing his infinite power cannot effect in us if only we go to him in humble and loving trust. When we go to him more humbly and with greater trust than had we not fallen, he will more than make up for the past. Indeed, he can make us a great saint in a moment, as he did with the Good Thief. It is the free gift of ourselves to him in loving trust and abandonment that determines how much his infinite power and loving mercy can do in us. Sanctity consists in living the truth, and the greatest truth is that God is all and the creature nothing of itself. The more we live that truth the greater will be our sanctity.

In the life of St. Gertrude we have a beautiful example of how Jesus can make up for our past losses. In the early years of her religious life Gertrude was more taken up with intellectual pursuits than with loving God. One day when she was lamenting the losses of those early years Jesus gave her to see her transformation into himself by a series of images. He showed her a little plant growing near his burning heart. But blighted by her faults and negligences, the plant shrank away until it resembled a cinder. As she invoked the mercy of Christ, streams of blood and water from his Sacred Heart revived the lifeless coal, which then assumed the form of a flowering tree, with branches that divided into three parts like a lily. Christ presented the tree to the Holy Trinity, and each of the three divine persons attached to one of the branches all the fruits that Gertrude would have produced had she corresponded perfectly to the inspirations of God's omnipotence, wisdom and love in those early years.

The closeness of our union with Jesus as God: Another aspect of our union with Jesus as God is its unimaginable closeness. In Jesus we are taken up into the very life of the Trinity: the fullness of all reality. In the Father is total Being, in the Son is all Truth and in the Holy Spirit is every lovable Good. United with Jesus we are taken up into his life within the Trinity, and so share in the fullness of Being, Truth and Love. When the Father knows and loves the Son and gives everything he is and has to his Son, he knows and loves us and gives everything he is to us in Jesus. And when the Son knows and loves the Father and returns everything back to him, we share with Jesus in so loving his Father through their mutual bond of love, the Holy Spirit. We have eternal life, the very life of God himself.

What the Father said of Jesus he can say of us, "This is my beloved Son in whom I am well pleased." (Mt. 17:5) And Jesus can say of us, "Father I have made your name known to them ... so that the love with which you loved me may be in them and so that I may be in them." (Jn. 17:26) And again, "I have given them the glory you gave to me that they maybe one as we are one. With me in them and you in me may they be so completely one that the world may realize that....I have loved them as much as you have loved me." (Jn. 17:22-23)

Mary, our perfect model and mother: In Mary we have a perfect model of how we should live with Jesus as God. Mary was perfectly united with Jesus in his love for his Father by accepting the Father's will in everything and by giving herself back to the Father with Jesus in total love. We see her perfect acceptance of the Father's will in her "Fiat" at the Annunciation and in all the happenings of divine providence in her life. We see it in her willingness to remain on earth after the Ascension of Jesus so as to mother the infant Church.

We find her giving everything back to the Father with Jesus in perfect faith, trust and love, especially in the supreme sacrifice of Jesus on Calvary. There she willingly sacrificed her motherly claim on Jesus and united herself with Jesus in his total gift of himself to his Father's will. Hence, she is a perfect model of our union with Jesus as God.

But she is also a loving mother who wants to help us love Jesus. She wants to help us find in Jesus our supreme happiness in receiving everything from the Father's love and in returning it all back to the Father enriched with our personal love. At the same time she wants to show us how to offer all of this for the salvation of all mankind.

D) THE MEASURE OF OUR SHARING IN THE PERFECTION OF JESUS AND MARY

In Jesus God has brought to perfection the greatest of his creative works. In Jesus' active redemption he has united our humanity with himself in the person of his divine Son in the most perfect possible union of love. And in Mary's passive redemption he has given one of our race the most perfect possible sharing in all that Christ has won for our humanity, so that no created person could be given and receive more than Mary has been given and received. In Jesus and Mary, God's great work of creation and redemption has reached an absolute perfection wholly worthy of God's infinite wisdom, power and goodness.

And now God is offering to every individual member of our human race a share in their absolute perfection, much as children share in all the riches and blessings of their parents. Whether individuals accept or reject what God is offering them in Jesus and Mary cannot detract from the absolute perfection of God's work; it only determines whether they will have a part in it or not, and to what degree. Now that degree is measured by the charity with which they accept and live God's offer of friendship as present in Jesus and Mary.

What is charity and its degree: What then is charity and what makes for its increase? In the first Part of this book (page 12) I mentioned that charity is to be identified with the love of benevolence: a love that gives and shares as opposed to the love of concupiscence by which one seeks something for himself. As creatures we only have what God has first given us. But when God gives to us, it is that we might have the joy of giving and sharing in our turn. God wants us to experience his own greater joy of giving and sharing. Hence, it is in giving that we grow in charity.

So as to give in our turn, we must first recognize the gifts God has given us in his creation, but especially in the spiritual and supernatural gift of his divine friendship in Jesus and Mary. Then, seeing God's great goodness and love in all these gifts, and realizing that he himself is far greater than any of his gifts, we will want to love and please him by using all his gifts in a return of love. If a king marries a peasant girl, he takes upon himself to provide her with all the riches required by her new rank. And the only thing he desires of her is that she should return everything back to him enriched with her personal love. So it is that we must love God with the love of charity or benevolence: a love that is willing to use and return everything we have received in order to please our Beloved.

The motivation behind charity is that one finds such joy in the goodness and greatness of his beloved that he seeks his own happiness more in the happiness of his beloved than in himself. Now the degree of such charity is measured by how much we are willing to sacrifice in order to please our Beloved.

As mentioned before, charity increases not directly by repeated acts but by an act that is more intense than any that went before it. This normally happens when some greater sacrifice is required of us in order to be faithful in our love for God in preference to our own pleasure.

How to judge our degree of charity: How can we know or judge our degree of charity? Certainly not by our feelings, for feelings are not wholly under our control, and our actions may not always conform to our feelings of love. By our actions? Yes, to some extent, but not wholly, for even success is no criterion of our love for God as the following example will show.

If I have a fault and I make a real effort to correct it and succeed, I will feel that I have been generous in loving God. But should I have the same fault, make the same effort and fail, I will feel that I have been wanting in generosity. However, it may be that God did not give me the extra help I needed to succeed because he saw I needed the humiliation. If, in that case, I accept the humiliation without giving up my determination to grow in love, I will be more pleasing to God than had I not failed.

Hence, the only absolute criterion of our degree of charity is our fully-determined will to love God with our whole heart, mind, and strength and our neighbor even as Jesus has loved us. A fully-determined will is the only thing that is wholly in my power and, if I persevere in it, in spite of every set back, I can be certain that God is pleased with me and that I am growing in charity. I can be sure that I am doing all God requires of me, and that is all I really need to know. Indeed, if we maintain that determined will, God will be able to do anything through us, once he sees that our humility can handle greater success.

Our supreme act of charity: Since charity grows and is measured by what we are willing to sacrifice in order to prove our love for God, the greater the good we are willing to sacrifice out of love for God the greater will be our charity. To be willing to sacrifice our very life for God is certainly the highest act of charity. That is why martyrdom is seen as the most perfect act of charity, according to those words of Jesus, "Greater love than this no man has that he should lay down his life for his friends." (Jn. 15:13)

While few of us will be called to be martyrs we can all freely accept our own death, however it may come, in loving submission to God's will and that can be just as perfect an act of love as martyrdom. If we can accept death at the hands of a persecutor, out of love for God, why can we not accept it at the hands of God's providence out of loving submission to his divine will? Hence, our death can and should be our supreme act of charity wherein we lovingly give back to God the very life he has given us, but now enriched with our personal love.

What is more, we can unite our death with that of Jesus himself in his supreme sacrifice of his life to the Father on the cross. When we do that it is really Jesus himself who dies in us his member. This is no mere pious wish, but a true reality. One day the mystic, Caryl Houselander, had a vision while walking down a city street. The whole horizon suddenly vanished before her and she saw Jesus in glory on the cross. After the vision had disappeared she happened to pass a newsstand and on the headline of the paper she read that the Czar of Russia had just been assassinated. In the picture of the Czar she recognized the features she had seen in the face of Christ on the cross. Jesus had died anew in the Czar. If that was true of the Czar, who was hardly a model Christian, how much more of one who is striving to love Jesus with all his heart.

Evidently, not everyone will reach the same degree of charity at the moment of their death. Hence, the saints in glory will differ from one another as the stars of heaven. However, everyone will share in the absolute perfection of Jesus and Mary even as all the children of a family share in all the love and blessings of their parents. All will thus receive the same reward, whether they were hired at the first or the eleventh hour, (cf. Mt. 20:9) but they will receive it according to their individual capacity. And that capacity is determined by their degree of charity. All will have that fullness of happiness they are capable of receiving. They will also share in the happiness of all their fellow members in Christ, even as the members of a family share in the joy and blessings of each and all its members. In heaven there will be no envy or regret, for the happiness of each will be complete in every way.

Our present life is a preparation for our future life: Our life in this world is but a preparation, a testing, a time of growth. Death will be the climax of that growth and fix it for all eternity in the degree of charity we have attained in the last act of our life.

In his death on the cross, Jesus' humanity was united with him in that eternal act whereby, as Son of God, he gives himself through the Holy Spirit, to the Father in the life of the Trinity. Dying in that act, his humanity, with all its members, is now forever united with him in his life within the Trinity. The more fully we are one with Jesus through charity, the more fully we will share in the glory of his humanity for all eternity. We will possess eternal life to the fullness of our capacity.

CHAPTER IV

THE FINAL FULFILLMENT OF GOD'S PLAN FOR CREATION

Now that we have seen how and to what degree we are called to share in God's own divine life, let us now consider some aspects of that perfect state of fulfillment of God's plan as it will exist for all eternity in heaven.

The first of these aspects is that of unity. Since God is a perfect unity in himself: a unity of three divine persons in one nature, he has willed that his creation, which came forth from him, should find its final fulfillment by coming back into unity with himself.

Another aspect of that final state of fulfillment, I will consider, is the nature of our sharing through Jesus and Mary in God's divine life in heaven. The third and final aspect is something Hans Von Balthazar has pointed out: that creation itself has been taken up into being a part of the mutual gift the three divine persons make of themselves to one another in the very life of the Trinity.

A) THAT ALL CREATION SHOULD COME BACK INTO UNITY WITH GOD

God in himself is the most perfect unity for he has the totality of all being without any parts or divisions. While he is three in persons he exists in only one divine nature: the great mystery of the Trinity.

If God has made the world to exist outside himself, it is only that, in the end it should come back into unity with himself in the most perfect possible way. That he has willed it so, is quite evident from those words of St. Paul, "Before the world was made he chose us, chose us in Christ to be holy and spotless...determining that we should be his adopted sons through Jesus Christ...he has let us know the mystery of his purpose ... that he would bring everything together under Christ as head, everything in the heavens and everything on earth. And it is in him that we are claimed as God's own." (Eph. 1:4-11)

This he has willed to effect in three stages.

1. By bringing the whole material creation into unity with man.
2. By bringing all mankind, with the material creation, into unity with Christ as man.
3. By bringing Christ, with all mankind and the material creation, into unity with himself in the divine life of the Trinity.

Stage 1 - All the material creation is taken up into unity with man: The material creation finds its purpose and fulfillment only in man; without man there would be no reason for its existence since it would be unknown except to God. But God knows it in himself more perfectly. Hence, it finds its purpose and reason for existing only in man and in serving man.

It serves man's body by providing him with food, clothing, shelter, and all his other bodily needs. It serves his intellectual life, for it is from the material creation that man derives all his intellectual concepts or knowledge whereby he can understand and reason and even come to know God as revealed in his works. It serves man also by offering him the means whereby he can pass on his knowledge to others by writing and other means of communication. It even serves man in his service of God by enhancing his liturgical celebrations.

In a deeper way creation is one with man in that man contains in himself all the different kingdoms of creation in miniature: the mineral kingdom, the vegetative kingdom, the animal kingdom and the rational kingdom. In this way man is a kind of microcosm of all creation.

What is more the material creation is made to serve man not only in this present life but also in his future life. St. Peter tells us, "We are waiting for what he promised: a new heaven and a new earth, a place where righteousness will be at home." (2 Pet. 3:13) And St. Paul writes, "Creation still retains the hope of being freed, like us from its slavery to decadence to enjoy the same freedom and glory as the children of God." (Rom. 8:20-21) When the blessed receive back their bodies at the general resurrection the renewed creation will be a source of joy to their bodily senses. They will have perfect joy not only in their spirits but also in their bodies. We have no way of knowing what this renewed creation will be like, but seeing the marvels of the present universe, we can be sure God's infinite wisdom and power and goodness will be more revealed in its renewal.

Stage 2 - All mankind is taken up into unity with Christ as man: While the material creation is taken up into man, man himself is taken up into unity with Christ to share in his divine life. Through sanctifying grace, we form one living organism with Christ: his Mystical Body. As man died to the divine life through Adam's sin, so now man is offered a new birth into the divine life in Christ. That is why St. Paul can say, "We are a new creation" a mankind living by the divine life present in Christ our head. When we accept baptism we are given birth into Christ. We become members of his Mystical Body which is the Church.

Christ is incomplete without all mankind: Every individual human person has a unique personality and special gifts which are a part of our universal humanity. No one, therefore, can possess the fullness of his humanity without a union of mutual knowledge and love with each and every other human person. Hence, Jesus really needs to be united with every individual human person in order to find his own personal perfect human happiness. And we need to be united with Jesus and with one another, in the same way, in order to find our own perfect human happiness. However, we all need Jesus in a very special way for only by being united with him can we enter into his unity with his Father in God's divine life.

As for those who are lost in hell, we can only say that, having freely chosen not to be a part of the new creation of mankind, they stand in relation to it as though they never existed. More we cannot know.

Stage 3 - In Jesus mankind and creation are taken up into unity with God: While creation is taken up into man and mankind is taken up into Christ as man, in the end both are taken up through Christ as God, into the life of the Trinity, so that God may be all in all. St. Paul tells us that, "From the beginning God chose us in Christ to be united with him as his sons and daughters."(cf. Eph. l:4-5) That is what the final effect of God's creation must bring about. Elsewhere God said, "The Word that goes forth from my mouth does not return to me empty, without carrying out my will and succeeding in what it was sent to do." (Isa. 55:11)

That all creation is to come back to God is clearly stated by St. Paul, "Then will come the end, when Christ will hand over the kingdom to God the Father, having done away with every sovereignty, authority and power, for Christ must be king until he has put all his enemies under his feet and the last enemy to be destroyed is death...and when everything is subject to him then the Son himself will be subject in his turn to the one who subjected all things to him, so that God may be all in all." (1 Cor. 15:24-28) As God is a unity in himself so all creation, having come forth from God will return to him in his Word, his divine Son, so that in the end God may again be all in all.

B) THE NATURE OF OUR UNITY WITH GOD IN JESUS AND MARY IN THE NEXT LIFE

1. As seen through social and organic comparisons: What our unity with God through Jesus and Mary in the next life will be like can be seen in the comparison of the family. We have seen that Jesus, in becoming man, has united mankind with himself much as the son of a king, by marrying a girl, takes her up into the royal family of his father, the king. Since Jesus is heir to the kingdom he is as a king himself; and his bride, Mary and the Church, become his queen while we, the members of Mary and the Church, are as their children, all united in the most perfect and loving family. Therein Jesus has the joy of being the most loving of Fathers to us his children, and we have the joy of having such a good and wonderful Father. Mary has the joy of being our Queen-mother and we the joy of having such a loving mother to present us to Jesus with all her motherly love. Together with Mary we will all be united with Jesus in his love for his Father through their own bond of mutual love, the Holy Spirit. We will be as one beautiful family wherein nothing will be wanting that we could possibly desire or need for the perfect happiness of all.

We can also consider our union with Jesus and Mary in the next life by the familiar comparisons of the vine with its branches and the soul with its body. However, since in these comparisons the united members are not all persons, their value is limited. Hence, we find Jesus using that comparison which exists between the three divine persons within the Trinity, "Father," Jesus says, "May they all be one; may they be one in us as you are in me and I am in you." (Jn. 17:21) When Philip asked Jesus, "Show us the Father." Jesus replied, "Do you not believe that I am in the Father and the Father in Me...the words I speak...are from the Father living in me who is doing this work." (Jn. 14:10) Here Jesus indicates that he, and therefore we in him, are so one with his Father that it is the Father who is living, speaking and acting in him and hence, also in us. It is as though we were truly God himself even as my body is truly myself. While we cannot push this unity to identity with God, still we cannot imagine how it is less than identity.

St. Thomas Aquinas tells us that the humanity of Jesus had no being other than the Being of God himself. It is the person that gives existence or being to every intellectual nature, for such a nature cannot exist except in a person. Since the humanity of Jesus has no person other then that of the Word of God, so it has **no being** other than the **Being of God**.

We have an analogy of this in ourselves. All the living cells in my body have a certain individuality of their own (which we may liken to being a person) and yet they have no existence apart from myself since they make up the one being or person who is me. In much the same way, we are all like living cells in Christ's Mystical Body and, while having our own individuality and person, we all make up the one Christ who is divine in his Being and Personality.

Indeed, if we see ourselves as the person of Christ's humanity, then, in the one Divine Being that exists in Jesus and his humanity, we have two persons: the Son of God and ourselves as his humanity, united in God's **Divine Being** much as the three divine persons are united in the Trinity. Thus is fulfilled, in a wondrous and ineffable way, that prayer of Jesus, "Father may they be one in us, as you are in me and I am in you." (Jn. 17:21) Here we see what God has done to make us gods in so far as that is possible to his infinite power.

2. As a partaker of the divine nature: While we have no way of fully knowing or experiencing what our union with God will be like in heaven, there is a scriptural text that may help. St. Peter tells us that through the gift of God we are, "Made partakers of God's divine nature." (2 Pet. 1:4) God cannot make us gods by nature, for we cannot be uncreated or independent. Hence, the next best he can do is to give us a participation in his divine nature or being. We can find some likeness to this in the way our human body participates in the intellectual life of our soul and in how Christ's humanity participates in his divinity by working miracles and the like. Just as we cannot imagine how our body could share more in the intellectual life of our soul without itself becoming intellectual or how Christ's humanity could share more in his divinity without becoming divine, so neither can we imagine how we can participate more in God's divine nature without ourselves becoming God.

Another comparison, which our imagination can appreciate, is that of iron plunged into fire. The iron participates so fully in the nature and beauty of the fire itself that it can hardly be distinguished from the fire. So we will share in the nature and the glory of God himself. We can put all this in words, but until we see and experience this unity with God in heaven we cannot appreciate the full meaning and reality of those words.

3. Some particular aspects of our union with God in heaven: Our union with God in eternity will, first of all, be eternal. For something to be eternal, it has to be so complete and perfect that nothing can be added or taken away from it. It must remain totally self-sufficient and unchangeable. Any change of increase or decrease means a movement that is measured by time. In heaven, then, our essential beatitude will consist in the vision of God and this will make us so one with God that nothing can be added or taken away from its fullness. Hence, it will be eternal, forever unchangeable.

To us such a state may appear stagnate, but that is only because we have never known a state that is so perfect that nothing is wanting to it, and so completely fulfilling that there is nothing more we could possibly imagine or desire. However, in the lesser joys of heaven there will be change and succession, and hence, a form of time, as for example in our communication with the saints and angels. Because of that, we will not exist wholly in eternity as is true of God. Hence, theologians generally use the term **aeveternity** to distinguish our final state from God's absolute eternity.

Another aspect of our union with God in heaven is that we will experience God's love for us in a unique and personal way. We will know and rejoice in the blessings of all the angels and saints in heaven, but that unique and personal union of each one with his God will be his own secret between God and himself alone. This is clearly indicated in the book of Revelation, "Those who prove victorious I will give a hidden manna and a white stone with a new name written on it, known only to the one who receives it." (Rev. 3:12) In heaven we will know the joy of community life in all its fullness and at the same time an intimate privacy with God and with anyone of the blessed whenever we may desire it. What is more, since we are one with Jesus as his bride, we can love the Father as much as Jesus himself loves the Father, and we are loved by the Father even as Jesus is loved by his Father.

Although the essential joy of heaven will be fixed and final for all eternity, there will be no boredom in that blessed place. In heaven we will find, not only every stable and lasting good in the infinite God, but also everything that is new and exciting. There we will find permanency in every possible good while at the same time the excitement of new discoveries without end. St. Augustine has captured this reality in the short phrase, "Ever ancient and ever new."

4. The lesser joys of heaven: What I have said so far about the future joy of heaven is known as the essential joy of heaven. But there are also lesser joys which we more easily relate to since they are experienced by our senses. These lesser joys are, however, so included in the essential joy of heaven that we would not miss them if we did not have them in their sensible form. But, because we are more conscious of these in our present life, we can appreciate them better and are more impressed by them.

We can be sure that no joy or happiness we can know in this life will be wanting in heaven, although such joys will be elevated, purified, and intensified to a supreme degree. There we will be united with all our loved ones and with all the saints and angels in the most perfect union of loving friendship without any fear of a future separation. We will have the fullness of all knowledge: nothing will be hidden from our understanding in any field of science, history or nature or anything else. All our senses will experience the greatest possible joy: the eye with beautiful sights, the ear with lovely sounds of harmony and music. Even our sense of smell, touch and taste will all have their highest possible satisfaction although it is difficult for us to imagine in what they will actually consist.

In our effort to understand these lesser joys of heaven we tend to amplify the created joys of this life and remove from them all present limitations and defects. But even should we take all the joys we have ever known in this life, put them all together in one moment and make that moment eternal, we will still be far from comprehending the joy that will be ours in our eternal home of heaven.

God is so great, so perfect and so loving that we cannot begin to imagine what it will be like to see him, to know him, to be united with him in an embrace of eternal love. In that embrace we will share in all his infinite riches and joy as a bride shares in all the glory, riches and tender love of her beloved, who here happens to be the king of the whole universe.

In that heavenly union, Jesus and Mary will always remain our mediators whereby it is made possible and perfect. Mary by uniting us with Jesus as man and Jesus by uniting us with his Father as God. Only Mary can unite us in perfect human friendship with Jesus and only Jesus can unite us. in perfect divine friendship with his Father and the Holy Spirit.

In Mary we can love Jesus even as we are loved by Jesus and in Jesus we can love the Father as perfectly as we are loved by the Father. Thus we will even have that greater joy of giving as much as we are given. While our union with Jesus through Mary, and through Jesus with God, will be absolutely perfect, still each one will share in it according to his own degree of charity, according to his capacity to receive that fullness of God's gifts imparted to us through Jesus and Mary.

C) CREATION: GOD'S GIFT TO HIMSELF

God's reason for creating was in order to share his life and happiness with others. Now God who lacks nothing cannot act in order to receive anything. Hence, God's great work of creation cannot, in any strict sense, be said to add anything to God or to his happiness. However, it is impossible for us to imagine that God does not at least find some added joy, as it were, in sharing his happiness with others. We know that even that cannot be, but we have no way of imagining how it cannot be so. We have to admit that there is a mystery here which we cannot, and need not, fully understand. Perhaps Hans Von Balthazar can give us some insight into this problem.

He sees the three divine persons of the Trinity putting their hand to creation as a kind of external gift of themselves to one another, somewhat as husband and wife seek to externalize their mutual love, in the birth of a child as a mutual gift of themselves to one another. Creation itself is thus taken up into the very life of the Trinity and becomes a part of their mutual love for one another, even as a child is taken up into the mutual love of husband and wife for each other.

The Father created us as a gift to his divine Son. Hence, those words of St. Paul, "Blessed be God the Father...who before the world was made...chose us in Christ, determining that we should become his adopted son...and that it is in him we are claimed as God's own." (Eph. 1:3-6)

The Son of God chose to create and redeem the world so as to give creation back to his Father in himself, as St. Paul indicates when he says, "When everything is subject to him, then the Son himself will be subject in his turn to the one who subjected all things to himself so that God might be all in all." (1. Cor. 15:28)

The Holy Spirit put his hand to creation also. That is why he is depicted in Genesis as hovering over creation, longing, as it were, to fill it with his own mutual love of Father and Son. He takes creation to himself, as being the child who, in an external way, unites the mutual love of Father and Son.

What is internal in God, his unity in mutual love, becomes external in creation which is then taken back into God to participate in his eternal life of love within the Trinity. All creation, summed up in man, is taken up by Christ into unity with God, as

Jesus prayed, "Father may they be one in us, as you are in me and I am in you." (Jn. 17:21)

Truly God has taken all creation back into himself in a way we shall never fully understand in this life. However, what we can know of it is so marvelous that we want to return his love in the most perfect possible way. And that he has given us the power to do in Jesus and Mary.

SUMMARY AND CONCLUSION

God has certainly revealed his greatness in the marvels of our material universe: in the vastness of the heavens, in the hidden wonders of the atom and in all living creatures. But God's greatness is still more revealed in that spiritual world of knowledge and love, as found in his intelligent creature: man:

Man and his spiritual nature: Man by reason of his spiritual powers of intellect and will, is far superior to all other creatures on earth, and it is by these powers that he has been made to the image and likeness of God. That is why God is man's true goal in whom alone man can find his final happiness and fulfillment.

In the present life, man finds his highest **natural** fulfillment in the mutual relationship of marriage and family life. But since man has the desire and the capacity to know all truth and goodness, he wants to be united in loving friendship with someone who is all truth and goodness, namely God. Hence, man's true and final goal, for which he was created, consists in being united with God in the highest possible union of mutual knowledge and love.

God achieves his goal with the utmost perfection: God created man for friendship with himself, but all that God does must be done with absolute perfection. Therefore God chose to offer the gift of his friendship to man in the highest possible way. This he has done through the Incarnation of his own divine Son by way of a twofold friendship: one with Jesus as man, in perfect human friendship, and the other with Jesus as God in perfect divine friendship.

In human friendship all mankind is united with Jesus as his bride **in Mary**, who, in Christ's mortal life, lived with him, in our place, a life of perfect human friendship. **In Jesus**, as God, all mankind, as his bride in Mary, is taken up with Jesus into perfect friendship with his Father.

Through Jesus' **active redemption**: his passion, death and resurrection, God has exhausted all he can give to a created nature. Through Mary's **passive redemption**: perfect reception, he has exhausted all that a mere creature can receive from God's fullness. In Jesus and Mary, God's work of creation and redemption has reached an absolute perfection wholly worthy of God's infinite wisdom, power and goodness.

We share in the fullness of Jesus and Mary: Being members of Jesus in his Mystical Body, we share in all that God has effected in Jesus and Mary; so much so, that what belongs to them is also ours, and can be freely used by us. This, our sharing in the riches of Jesus and Mary is a reality not only for this present life: in order to grow in charity, but also in the future life of heaven: wherein we will share in their reward and glory.

How we share in the gifts and graces of Jesus and Mary in this life: In our present life we are free to use all the riches and graces of Jesus and Mary as being our very own. Jesus and Mary have attained their final goal and so they can no longer grow in charity and merit. But we, their members, who are still in this world, can use their riches and graces as our own so as to grow in charity and merit ourselves. In this way, we the members of Christ's Mystical Body, enter ever more fully into all the riches of Jesus our head.

The extent to which every individual uses the riches of Jesus and Mary will determine their own degree of charity. And that degree of charity arises from two things: **first** from their free acceptance of all God is giving them in Jesus and Mary, and **secondly** from the extent to which they live out that acceptance in their daily life through faith, hope and charity.

How we should live out our acceptance of God's gifts in Jesus and Mary: The most basic truth that a creature must live in its relationship with God is that the creature is nothing of itself without God, and that God is the only source of every good it can receive. To live that truth in our relationship with God is very important. It consists in doing two things: **first**, in dying to ourselves, and **secondly**, in living wholly for God as our supreme good.

Dying to ourselves requires that we come to the conviction that without God we are of ourselves nothing but rebellion, refusal, and negation. But we are to come to that conviction, not so much by any personal effort, as by humbly accepting all the experiences God sends us of our weakness, blindness, failures and sinfulness. These negative experiences are of great value for they help us to grow in humility: convincing us of our true relationship with God.

Dying to self is only the negative aspect of living our true relationship with God. Its positive aspect consists in loving and seeking God alone as our supreme good. This we are moved to do, especially by seeing how much God has loved us in spite of our nothingness and misery and sinfulness. We are then prompted to love him in return with all our heart, mind, soul and strength. This we seek to do, not so much according to our own plans and desires, but by being perfectly docile and faithful in fulfilling God's will as it comes to us through the commandments, the duties of our state in life, the arrangements of his providence and those inner inspirations that are clearly from God. At the same time we will prove our love of Jesus by loving our neighbor, knowing, as Jesus has said, "What you do to one of these least of my brethren you do to me." (Mt. 25:40)

If we keep our habitual will set on seeking everything in God and on striving to love God in himself and in our neighbor, we will be growing in charity even though we may not think so. We can not really know our degree of charity, nor is that necessary. All we need to know is that our determined will is set according to the truth, and that we are trying to live that truth. When we do that then it will be Jesus loving his Father in us, and we will come to share in Jesus' own merits and glory.

How we will share in the gifts of Jesus and Mary in heaven: If we can use all the riches and graces of Jesus and Mary as being our own in this life, in the next life we will enter into their reward and glory as being our own. Since what God has achieved in Jesus and Mary is absolutely perfect, all the blessed in heaven will enjoy their reward and glory. All will have the same reward as Jesus and

Mary, whether they were called at the first or the eleventh hour. (cf. Mt. 20:9) However, each will possess it according to his own personal capacity determined by his degree of charity. Thus God's work of creation will have reached absolute perfection in itself, a work wholly worthy of God's infinite wisdom, power and goodness, yet each of the blessed with share in it according to his personal capacity. All the blessed will differ in glory even as the stars in heaven differ in brightness.

How will the blessed share in the reward and glory of Jesus and Mary? Certainly not in some abstract or general way, as for example, the way all the spectators share in a ball game or a movie. No, it will be in a very personal and loving way, much as children share in all the gifts and riches of their parents, through the parents' own personal and loving solicitude for their children. It will be as Jesus said of the faithful servants whom the master finds watching, "He will sit them down at table and wait on them." (Lk. 12:37)

Mary is unique and supreme: Mary unites us perfectly with Jesus and Jesus unites us perfectly with his Father. Jesus is unique, as a man who is truly God, and Mary is unique, as that creature who is perfectly united with Jesus; the man who is God. Mary is unique as being the absolutely perfect bride of Christ: the one who has received all that a creature can be given. Mary is also unique as being saved by prevention so that she was never stained by even the slightest defect or sin. That is why Scripture can speak of Mary as being unique and perfect. "One is my dove; my perfect one is but one; she is the darling of her mother, the favorite of the one who bore her." (Cant. 6:8) "Many women have done admirable things, but you surpass them all."(Prov. 31:29)

Abraham, because of his faith, received the promise that "In his seed all the nations of the earth would be blessed." (Gen. 22:18) Mary, because of her faith, was moved by the Holy Spirit to sing, "All generations will call me blessed." (Lk. 1:48).Abraham, by reason of his seed was to be a blessing to all the nations. Mary, by reason of her offspring, is that blessing: that perfect creature living by the life of God. As such, Mary is called blessed by all the generations of mankind as its supreme ideal, its highest glory, its greatest hero, and queenly mother. Hence, she is rightly praised as, "The most exalted daughter of mankind, the greatest glory of the Church, the deepest joy of the Christian people, and the highest honor of our race." (cf. Jud. 15:9) Mary is God's **Supreme Masterpiece**, but as our Mother she is the **Mediatrix of all graces**.